丽江师范高等专科学校资助出版

英力克英语经典影片教程

主　编　张庆梅　段平华　唐　湖
副主编　谷　兰　杨慧梅　朱　俊
参　编　徐金义　杨丽萍　邓丽萍

苏州大学出版社

图书在版编目(CIP)数据

英力克英语经典影片教程 / 张庆梅,段平华,唐湖主编. -- 苏州：苏州大学出版社,2023.7
ISBN 978-7-5672-4459-7

Ⅰ.①英… Ⅱ.①张…②段…③唐… Ⅲ.①英语-口语-自学参考资料 Ⅳ.①H319.9

中国国家版本馆CIP数据核字(2023)第118212号

书　　名：英力克英语经典影片教程

YINGLIKE YINGYU JINGDIAN YINGPIAN JIAOCHENG

主　　编：张庆梅　段平华　唐　湖
责任编辑：金莉莉
装帧设计：刘　俊

出版发行：苏州大学出版社(Soochow University Press)
社　　址：苏州市十梓街1号　邮编：215006
印　　刷：江苏图美云印刷科技有限公司
邮购热线：0512-67480030
销售热线：0512-67481020

开　　本：787 mm×1 092 mm　1/16　印张：13.25　字数：315千
版　　次：2023年7月第1版
印　　次：2023年7月第1次印刷
书　　号：ISBN 978-7-5672-4459-7
定　　价：68.00元

图书若有印装错误,本社负责调换
苏州大学出版社营销部　电话：0512-67481020
苏州大学出版社网址　http://www.sudapress.com
苏州大学出版社邮箱　sdcbs@suda.edu.cn

　　随着高等教育国际化的不断推进，中国学生英语学习需求也呈现出多元化和多层次的发展趋势。为了满足这些需求，编写组依据《教育部办公厅关于加强高等学历继续教育教材建设与管理的通知》（教职成厅函〔2021〕28号）和《中华人民共和国国民经济和社会发展第十四个五年规划和2035年远景目标纲要》的指导和要求，结合现代外语教学理论和实践，编写了这本《英力克英语经典影片教程》。

　　《英力克英语经典影片教程》是一本全新的英语影视实训教材，专为英语学习者量身打造。本教材将英语学习和经典电影文化相结合，不仅有助于提高学生的英语水平，还能够拓展他们的文化视野，为他们提供一个身临其境的英语学习机会。在编写本教材时，编者特别注重培养学生的两种语言能力。一方面，通过欣赏影片，引导学生借助电影中所呈现的情景和人物角色进行语言交际实践；另一方面，通过影片主题进行辩论活动，锻炼学生运用英语进行辩论的能力。通过与英语电影精彩片段的互动，学生不仅能够感受英语的魅力，还能够在自然的情境中习得语言。

　　本教材的一个非常重要的特色在于课程思政贯穿教材始终。结合中国特色社会主义的本质要求，编者将课程思政融入英语学习中。不再是单纯的知识传授，而是注重培养学生爱国情怀和社会责任感，努力让学生在学习英语的同时树立正确的人生观、世界观和价值观。同时，本教材提供了精心选取的影视片段和相应的学习材料，设定了相应的主题和任务，引领学生探索和思考现实生活中的问题。此外，本教材还将文化元素和语言学习紧密结合，提供了许多配套的练习以及实用的学习技巧和策略，旨在帮助学生消除语言障碍，更好地了解和欣赏英语国家的文化，提高跨文化交际能力，使他们能够在全球范围内更好地交流和实现自己的人生价值。

　　本教材采用了先进的CBI（Content-Based Instruction）教学理念，即以内容为基础的教学理念，旨在为英语学习者提供一种全方位、多元化的英语习得方式。影视资源的引入，致力于让学生在英语学习的过程中接触到更多的文化。同时，本教材也注重语言的习得，采用了斯蒂芬·克拉申的"习得"理论。

在本教材的编写过程中，编者还注重对"英力克英语语言习得模式"的创新。该模式将影视材料作为主要素材，通过声音、图像、场景等全方位的呈现方式，营造出生动的英语语言环境，让学生在真实的语言输入环境中，通过模仿和自我发现，自然习得语言、技能和知识，避免了过多机械、死记硬背的语言学习方式，帮助学生更好地提升英语语言技能。

本教材包含18个单元，采用了不同难度级别的电影片段。直观的画面、真实的对话和丰富的情境，让学生在感受语言的美妙之余，能够了解英语的实际运用场景。每个章节还有一些提炼的经典的电影台词，以及在各种场景下的交际练习，希望能帮助学生更好地掌握英语。

希望本教材能够帮助广大的英语学习者提高他们的英语语感和语言表达能力，让他们在世界舞台上更加自信地展示自己，在国际视野下更加积极地参与建设美好的人类社会。与此同时，本教材得到了教育专家的指导和支持，专家的丰富经验和专业知识让本教材更加丰满、深入，为学生提供了更加优质的英语学习体验。相信本教材将给学生的英语语言学习和英语教师的英语教学带来实质性的提升。希望本教材能得到广大学生和教育工作者的认可和喜爱。让我们共同努力，一起推动英语教育的发展。

华东师范大学

花　蓉

# 教学指南

为了用好本教材,师生在使用此教材开展教学之前,有必要研读并熟悉以下内容。

一、编写理念和教学模式

第一,本教材的编写理念基于"英力克英语习得模式"。英力克是英文 EANLIC(English Acquired as a "Native" Language in China)的中文音译,是丽江师范高等专科学校外国语学院于 2004 年首创的一种英语习得模式,其核心是要在中国这样一个非英语国家的一定时间、空间和人群范围内,人为地创造出一种类似于将英语作为母语的语言运用环境,使学生在课堂学习英语的同时,结合课内和课外的语言环境自然习得英语,最终达到熟练运用英语进行交际的目的。为了创建一个良好的英语语言环境,保证充足的语言输入量与输出量,该模式强调将课内教学与课外学习有机、无缝地衔接起来,强调即学即用、学用结合,强调英语学习的生活化、日常化、内涵化、情景化、趣味化。

第二,本教材针对的是英语口语教学,设计理念和体系也是根据英力克英语口语的教学环节和步骤实施的,是"英力克英语习得模式"基本理念的集中体现。英力克英语口语课程有三个重要的环节:第一个环节是英语日的英语交流(Routine English Communication),在每周四全天,要求学生之间、学生与英语老师之间用英语进行日常交流;第二个环节是英语午谈(English Chat),学生针对所学影片的问题进行小组讨论;第三个环节是英力克晚会(EANLIC Party),由学生结合所学影片的主题,在老师的指导下完成方案,并用英文举办一场丰富多彩的英语晚会。

第三,本教材体现了 CBI(Content-based Instruction)的教学理念。CBI 突出外语的工具性特点,强调语言学习的综合性和整体性,强调通过外语的实际运用习得语言。因此,虽然这门课程的名称是"英力克英语口语",却远不止口语训练本身,涉及了听、说、读、写、译等各方面的综合学习,涉及了中西方文化的对比、跨文化交际意识的培养和提升,涉及了很多背景知识的学习。

第四,利用本教材进行的课程教学还体现了翻转课堂(Flipped Classroom)的教学特点。由于学习内容的丰富性,而课堂上老师可直接支配的时间又极其有限,这就要求学生

在课前和课后完成大量的自学任务,否则教学效果就要大打折扣。老师上课时主要检验学生学习的效果,解答疑难问题,引导学生深入思考,并督促学生完成相关的学习任务。

第五,利用本教材进行的课程教学完全体现了"以学生为中心"的教学理念,即课程教学过程的主角是学生而非老师。不论是英语日的英语交流、英语午谈,还是英力克晚会,都是由学生任主角,任课教师则扮演评价者、助手、观察者、参与者等角色。

二、编写体系和教学建议

本教材共有18个单元,共有 *Mulan*，*The Lion King* 等18部英文影片。每个单元都有 Pre-class Tasks(课前任务)、In-class Tasks(课中任务)、English Chat Task(英语午谈任务)、EANLIC Party Tasks(英力克晚会任务)、After-class Tasks(课后任务)、References(参考资料)几个部分。在使用这几个部分时,需要注意如下事项。

1. Section Ⅰ　Pre-class Tasks

学生要按照要求提前认真看至少2~3遍影片,否则后面的教学将很难正常进行。多看英文原版电影为学生提供一种最接近真实英语语言应用的环境,能提高学生英语语感和语言综合能力。第一遍以理解剧情内容为主,可以看中英文双语脚本的影片,第二遍、第三遍则要特别关注剧情的细节,要尽可能地根据剧情的发展揣摩、理解和记忆英文单词和句子的意思。这个部分里所列的单词和句子仅仅是对学生的最低要求,学生可以根据自己的基础和学习能力加量。

2. Section Ⅱ　In-class Tasks

如果课堂教学时间紧张,可以把 Workshop 这个部分布置为学生的课前任务,提前以小组为单位进行讨论。这个部分不仅有用于检验学生对影片的理解程度的问题,还配有相应的句型,丰富学生的表达方式。其他几个部分可以由老师根据上课时间灵活处理。

3. Section Ⅲ　English Chat Task

英语午谈一般都是在室外进行的小组讨论,讨论的内容主要涉及影片的 themes(主题),如果时间允许,还可以把 Workshop 里的问题再拿出来进行讨论。

在各小组讨论的过程中,老师可以深入各个小组检查和评估学生的讨论效果,也可以组织各小组相互交叉检查,最后再将讨论结果汇总到老师那;英语午谈作为教学环节的一个有机组成部分,老师须严格把控时间,保证口语训练的效率,有效避免传统"英语角"的松散和不可持续性问题。

4. Section Ⅳ　EANLIC Party Tasks

这个部分须在老师的指导下,由学生精心准备方案和PPT,经老师审核通过后,小组轮流用英文组织开展。其组织形式和内容安排相对灵活,可以充分发挥学生的创造力,做到教育性、开放性和趣味性相统一。在晚会结束之前,应留15分钟左右的时间给老师和同学进行晚会点评和教学总结，开展英力克晚会的英语交流表现自评或互评，并安排相关课后任务。

5. Section Ⅴ　After-class Tasks

这个部分是教学的课后延伸，有利于学生对相关知识的巩固和延伸，要求学生根据任务要求在课后完成。

6. References

这个部分是为了方便师生查阅和学习有关内容，主要涉及叙事结构和辩论技巧两个方面，在教学各环节均可灵活使用。

总之，本教材遵循了先进的编写理念，并采用了对应的编写体系、适合的教学模式和教学方法，相信老师们一定能教有所悟，同学们一定能学有所得！

最后，华东师范大学外语学院的朱晓映老师和花蓉老师在教材的编写过程中给予了很多指导和无私的帮助，特借此机会向她们表示由衷的感谢和崇高的敬意！

段平华

目录

Unit 1 *Mulan* (1998) / 001

Unit Objectives: / 001
Section I　Pre-class Tasks　/ 002
Section II　In-class Tasks　/ 005
Section III　English Chat Task　/ 008
Section IV　EANLIC Party Tasks　/ 009
Section V　After-class Tasks　/ 010
References　/ 010

Unit 2　*The Lion King 1*　/ 014

Unit Objectives: / 014
Section I　Pre-class Tasks　/ 015
Section II　In-class Tasks　/ 017
Section III　English Chat Task　/ 020
Section IV　EANLIC Party Tasks　/ 021
Section V　After-class Tasks　/ 022
References　/ 022

Unit 3　*Kung Fu Panda 1*　/ 025

Unit Objectives: / 025
Section I　Pre-class Tasks　/ 026
Section II　In-class Tasks　/ 028
Section III　English Chat Task　/ 031
Section IV　EANLIC Party Tasks　/ 031

Section V   After-class Tasks   / 032
References   / 032

Unit 4   *Brother Bear 1*   / 034

Unit Objectives：/ 034
Section I   Pre-class Tasks   / 035
Section II   In-class Tasks   / 038
Section III   English Chat Task   / 041
Section IV   EANLIC Party Tasks   / 042
Section V   After-class Tasks   / 042
References   / 043

Unit 5   *Ice Age 1*   / 045

Unit Objectives：/ 045
Section I   Pre-class Tasks   / 046
Section II   In-class Tasks   / 049
Section III   English Chat Task   / 051
Section IV   EANLIC Party Tasks   / 052
Section V   After-class Tasks   / 053
References   / 053

Unit 6   *Charlotte's Web*   / 056

Unit Objectives：/ 056
Section I   Pre-class Tasks   / 057
Section II   In-class Tasks   / 059
Section III   English Chat Task   / 062
Section IV   EANLIC Party Tasks   / 064
Section V   After-class Tasks   / 064
References   / 065

Unit 7   *Coco*   / 067

Unit Objectives：/ 067
Section I   Pre-class Tasks   / 068

Section II　In-class Tasks　／070

Section III　English Chat Task　／073

Section IV　EANLIC Party Tasks　／074

Section V　After-class Tasks　／074

References　／075

Unit 8　Colorful Yunnan Tourism Paradise　／077

Unit Objectives：／077

Section I　Pre-class Tasks　／078

Section II　In-class Tasks　／080

Section III　English Chat Task　／083

Section IV　EANLIC Party Tasks　／084

Section V　After-class Tasks　／085

References　／085

Unit 9　Wild China (Episode 1, Heart of the Dragon)　／089

Unit Objectives：／089

Section I　Pre-class Tasks　／090

Section II　In-class Tasks　／093

Section III　English Chat Task　／096

Section IV　EANLIC Party Tasks　／097

Section V　After-class Tasks　／098

References　／098

Unit 10　Blue Planet II (Episode 1)　／101

Unit Objectives：／101

Section I　Pre-class Tasks　／102

Section II　In-class Tasks　／105

Section III　English Chat Task　／108

Section IV　EANLIC Party Tasks　／109

Section V　After-class Tasks　／110

References　／110

Unit 11 Green Book / 114

Unit Objectives：/ 114
Section I   Pre-class Tasks   / 115
Section II   In-class Tasks   / 117
Section III   English Chat Task   / 120
Section IV   EANLIC Party Tasks   / 120
Section V   After-class Tasks   / 121
References   / 121

Unit 12 Forrest Gump / 124

Unit Objectives：/ 124
Section I   Pre-class Tasks   / 125
Section II   In-class Tasks   / 128
Section III   English Chat Task   / 130
Section IV   EANLIC Party Tasks   / 131
Section V   After-class Tasks   / 131
References   / 132

Unit 13 The Sound of Music / 134

Unit Objectives：/ 134
Section I   Pre-class Tasks   / 135
Section II   In-class Tasks   / 138
Section III   English Chat Task   / 141
Section IV   EANLIC Party Tasks   / 142
Section V   After-class Tasks   / 142
References   / 143

Unit 14 The Shawshank Redemption / 145

Unit Objectives：/ 145
Section I   Pre-class Tasks   / 146
Section II   In-class Tasks   / 149
Section III   English Chat Task   / 152

Section IV　EANLIC Party Tasks　/ 153
Section V　After-class Tasks　/ 153
References　/ 153

Unit 15　Life Is Beautiful　/ 157

Unit Objectives：/ 157
Section I　Pre-class Tasks　/ 158
Section II　In-class Tasks　/ 161
Section III　English Chat Task　/ 163
Section IV　EANLIC Party Tasks　/ 164
Section V　After-class Tasks　/ 164
References　/ 165

Unit 16　Gone with the Wind　/ 167

Unit Objectives：/ 167
Section I　Pre-class Tasks　/ 168
Section II　In-class Tasks　/ 170
Section III　English Chat Task　/ 174
Section IV　EANLIC Party Tasks　/ 175
Section V　After-class Tasks　/ 175
References　/ 175

Unit 17　Pride and Prejudice (2005)　/ 178

Unit Objectives：/ 178
Section I　Pre-class Tasks　/ 179
Section II　In-class Tasks　/ 181
Section III　English Chat Task　/ 184
Section IV　EANLIC Party Tasks　/ 185
Section V　After-class Tasks　/ 185
References　/ 186

Unit 18　*Jane Eyre* (2011)　/ 188

Unit Objectives：/ 188

Section I　Pre-class Tasks　/ 189

Section II　In-class Tasks　/ 191

Section III　English Chat Task　/ 194

Section IV　EANLIC Party Tasks　/ 194

Section V　After-class Tasks　/ 195

References　/ 195

参考文献　/ 198

Unit 1

Mulan (1998)

Unit Objectives:

1. Speaking skills:
   - Acquire the ability to retell a story using the hero's journey format.
   - Learn the proper method to initiate a debate with a suitable format.
2. Emotional objectives:
   - Cultivate students' courage to overcome difficult situations in life.
   - Foster a sense of love and devotion towards their homeland.
   - Strengthen the bond within families.

Section I Pre-class Tasks

The students are supposed to watch the movie of *Mulan* (1998) for at least 2 or 3 times ahead of the class, the first time for general understanding of the movie, and the second and third times for more detailed understanding and learning of English language, and then complete the following tasks before the class time.

☞ 1. Classic movie lines

Direction: *Read and recite the following lines from the movie.*

(1) A single grain of rice can tip the scale. One man may be the difference between victory and defeat.

(2) The flower that blooms in adversity is the most rare and beautiful of all.

(3) The fate of yourself rests in your claws.

☞ 2. Background knowledge

Direction: *Go through the passage and prepare to share the information in class.*

The movie begins with Fa Mulan nervously preparing for her meeting with the matchmaker. For young girls in ancient China, marrying a good husband and bearing children is the way to bring honour to a family.

The news comes that China is under attack from the Hun army. The emperor issues constriction orders to draft one man from each family to form imperial army to fight in the war. Mulan's father has more than once served the army, but now he is aged and weak. Knowing her father might die if he were to fight another war, Mulan decides to disguise as a man to join the army in her father's place without anyone knowing. Because women are not allowed to join the army, Mulan would be executed if her identity were to be exposed. Her parents have no choice but to pray for the protection from the ancestors of the Fa family. The spirits of the Fa family hold a meeting and decide to send Mushu, a small dragon, the family guardian to protect Mulan.

Mulan arrives at the military camp and serves under Shang, a young officer from a military family. Mulan begins hard military training, during which she seeks to keep her identity from being revealed with the help of Mushu and the lucky cricket. Gradually, she wins friendship, respect and recognition from the fellow soldiers.

In a combat with Shan Yu's army, Mulan creates an avalanche and saves the imperial army, but exposes her identity. Shang gets the order from Chi-Fu, the councilman of the emperor that he should execute Mulan immediately. Shang refuses to obey the order and leaves her to her own devices.

Shan and his troops return to the imperial city, and they are welcomed as heroes. However, Mulan discovers that Shan Yu and the major forces of his army survived the avalanche and plans to take the imperial city. Mulan runs to the imperial city to warn Shang. But Shang and others don't take Mulan's words seriously, because they despise Mulan as a liar.

Shan Yu seizes the emperor and threatens to kill him if he refuses to bow to him and accepts him as the new leader of China. The emperor socially refuses. Mulan turns the tide by revealing Shan Yu's conspiracy with enormous firework display. With the help of Mulan, the emperor is saved and Shan Yu is defeated.

Despite her fraud, the emperor offers her the position of the councilman as a reward. Mulan declines and chooses to return home to her parents.

Mulan brings honour to her family through fighting bravely and saving the country and the people.

3. Vocabulary

Direction: *Learn these new words and expression(s) from this movie and try to use them at EANLIC night.*

troop /truːp/ *n.* [pl.] soldiers in an organized group 部队,军队

conscription /kənˈskrɪpʃn/ *n.* when people are made to join the army, navy etc. 征兵

demure /dɪˈmjʊə(r)/ *adj.* quiet, serious, and well-behaved, used especially about women in the past 端庄娴静的(尤指旧时妇女)

refined /rɪˈfaɪnd/ *adj.* (of a person) polite and well-educated; having the sort of manners that are considered typical of a high social class 有礼貌的,优雅的,有教养的

punctual /ˈpʌŋktʃuəl/ *adj.* arriving, happening, or being done at exactly the time that has been arranged 准时的,守时的,如期的

matchmaker /ˈmætʃmeɪkə(r)/ *n.* someone who tries to find a suitable partner for someone else to marry 媒人

primp /prɪmp/ *v.* to make yourself look attractive by arranging your hair, putting on make-up, etc. 梳妆打扮

polish /ˈpɒlɪʃ/ *v.* to make something smooth, bright, and shiny by rubbing it 擦亮,擦光

instant /ˈɪnstənt/ *adj.* happening or produced immediately 立刻的,速成的

hairdo /ˈheəduː/ *n.* hair style 发型

obedient /əˈbiːdiənt/ *adj.* always doing what you are told to do, or what the law, a rule etc. says you must do 服从的,顺从的,听话的

breeding /ˈbriːdɪŋ/ *n.* the fact of coming from a family of a high rank and having polite social behavior 教养

uproot /ˌʌpˈruːt/ *v.* to pull a plant and its roots out of the ground 把(植物)连根拔起

undertaker /ˈʌndəteɪkə(r)/ *n.* someone whose job is to arrange funerals 殡葬人员,殡仪员

clumsy /ˈklʌmzi/ *adj.* moving or doing things in a careless way, especially so that you drop things, knock into things, etc. 笨拙的,不灵活的

disgrace /dɪsˈɡreɪs/ *n.* the loss of other people's respect because you have done something they strongly disapprove of 丢脸,耻辱,出丑

proclamation /ˌprɒkləˈmeɪʃn/ *n.* an official public statement about something that is important, or when someone makes such a statement 公告,声明(书),宣言

invade /ɪnˈveɪd/ *v.* to enter a country, town, or area using military force, in order to take control of it 武力入侵,侵略,侵占

salvation /sælˈveɪʃn/ *n.* something that prevents or saves someone or something from danger, loss, or failure 解救物,救星,救助者

masquerade /ˌmæskəˈreɪd/ *n.* a way of behaving or speaking that hides your true thoughts or feelings 伪装,掩饰

penalty /ˈpenəlti/ *n.* a punishment for breaking a law, rule, or legal agreement (因违反法律、规则或合约而受到的)惩罚,处罚

lizard /ˈlɪzəd/ *n.* a type of reptile that has four legs and a long tail 蜥蜴

tattoo /təˈtuː/ *n.* a picture or writing that is permanently marked on your skin using a needle and ink 文身

tranquil /ˈtræŋkwɪl/ *adj.* pleasantly calm, quiet, and peaceful 平静的,宁静的,静谧的

typhoon /taɪˈfuːn/ *n.* a very violent tropical storm 台风

cannon /ˈkænən/ *n.* a large heavy powerful gun that was used in the past to fire heavy metal balls (旧时的)大炮,加农炮

snatch /snætʃ/ *v.* to take something away from someone with a quick, often violent, movement 抢去,强夺,攫取

treason /ˈtriːzn/ *n.* the crime of being disloyal to your country or its government, especially by helping its enemies or trying to remove the government using violence 叛国(罪),通敌(罪)

fraud /frɔːd/ *n.* someone or something that is not what it is claimed to be 骗子,骗局

concubine /ˈkɒŋkjubaɪn/ *n.* a woman in the past who lived with and had sex with a man who already had a wife or wives, but who was socially less important than the wives (旧时的)妾,姨太太,小老婆

pompous /ˈpɒmpəs/ *adj.* someone who is pompous thinks that they are important, and shows this by being very formal and using long words—used to show disapproval 虚夸的,言辞浮夸的

impersonate /ɪmˈpɜːsəneɪt/ *v.* to pretend to be someone else by copying their appearance, voice, and behavior, especially in order to deceive people (尤指为行骗而)假扮,假冒(他人)

adversity /ədˈvɜːsəti/ *n.* a situation in which you have a lot of problems that seem to be caused by bad luck 逆境,不幸,厄运

Expression(s)

take a chance 碰碰运气;冒险;投机;利用一下机会(亦作 take chances)

☞ 4. Character description

Direction: *Describe the main characters by using at least 5 adjectives in this movie with the* reference of the words you have learned, and find examples in the movie to support your ideas (Table 1.1).

Table 1.1 Main Characters in *Mulan* (1998)

Main Characters	Adjectives	Examples
Mulan		
Mulan's family		
Li Shang		
Chi-Fu		
Emperor		
Mushu		

Section II In-class Tasks

☞ 1. Workshop

Direction: *Discuss the questions with your classmates, and use the following sentence structures if it is possible.*

Sentence structures
- According to the movie, we can reasonably infer ...
- Based on the movie, it could convey that ...
- The movie suggests that the primary solution for a problem ...
- The movie seems to imply that ...

(1) Why is it important for Mulan and others in the movie not to shame their families?
(2) Why do the ancestors care about what happens to Mulan?
(3) Why is it a crime for a woman to enlist in the army?
(4) Who is your favourite character in this movie? Why?
(5) How can a girl bring honour to her family?
(6) Mulan's father gets the order to serve in the army to protect his country. How does he feel about it?
(7) When and how do others find out the truth about Mulan's identity?
(8) Why does Mulan leave home at night without anyone knowing?
(9) Think about the role of women in ancient China. What are the standards for a good daughter and a good wife?
(10) Compare Mulan with other women. How is she different from others?

☛ 2. Cloze

Direction: *Fill in the gaps in the following passage and dialogue taken from the movie with the words or phrases given below.*

■ **Passage**

| beautiful | staring straight back | blooms | pass for | break |
| reflection | meant | bride | hide | blossoms |

Look at me. I will never ___1___ a perfect ___2___ or a perfect daughter. Can it be I'm not ___3___ to play this part? Now I see that if I were truly to be myself, I would ___4___ my family's heart. Who is that girl I see, ___5___ at me? Why is my ___6___ someone I don't know? Somehow I cannot ___7___ who I am, though I've tried. When will my reflection show who I am inside?

What beautiful ___8___ we have this year! But look. This one's late. But I'll bet that when it ___9___, it will be the most ___10___ of all.

■ **Dialogue**

armor	See to it	fight	deliberate	dynasty
allowed	pompous	positions	adversity	mess
deceived	respect	rare	impersonated	take

Chi Fu: That was a ___1___ attempt on my life!
Where is she? Now she's done it.
What a ___2___! Stand aside!
That creature's not worth protecting.

Li Shang: She's a hero.

Chi Fu: 'Tis a woman. She'll never be worth anything.

Li Shang: Listen, you ___3___...

Emperor: That is enough.

Li Shang: Your Majesty, I can explain.

Emperor: I've heard a great deal about you, Fa Mulan. You stole your father's ___4___, ran away from home, ___5___ a soldier, ___6___ your commanding officer, the Chinese army, destroyed my palace … and … you have saved us all.

Mushu: My little baby is all grown up and … and savin' China. You have a tissue?

Emperor: Chi Fu.

Chi Fu: Your Excellency?

Emperor: ___7___ that this woman is made a member of my council.

Chi Fu: Member ... what? But ... There are no council ___8___ open, Your Majesty.
Emperor: Very well. You can have his job.
Chi Fu: What? I ... Oh.
Mulan: With all due ___9___, Your Excellency, I think I've been away from home long enough.
Emperor: Then ... ___10___ this, so your family will know what you have done for me. And this, so the world will know what you have done for China.
Yao: Is she ___11___ to do that?
Li Shang: Um ... you ... You ___12___ good.
Mulan: Oh. Thank you. Khan, let's go home.
Emperor: The flower that blooms in ___13___ is the most ___14___ and beautiful of all.
Li Shang: Sir?
Emperor: You don't meet a girl like that every ___15___.

☞ 3. Story retelling

Direction: *Study the information in Reference 1 on hero's journey of this unit, and then retell the story of* Mulan (1998) *by using specific details to support your ideas (Table 1.2).*

Table 1.2 12 Stages of Mulan's Journey

Stages	Mulan's Journey
Ordinary world	
Call to adventure	
Refusal of the call	
Meeting the mentor	
Crossing the threshold	
Trials and tests	
Approach to innermost cave	
The ordeal	
The reward	
The road back	
Th resurrection	
Return with the elixir	

☞ 4. Sentence rearrangement

Direction: *Put the following sentences into the chronological order based on the story of Mulan* (*Table 1.3*).

Table 1.3 Sentences from *Mulan* (1998)

Orders	Sentences
	A single grain of rice can tip the scale. One man may be the difference between victory and defeat.
	Don't worry, Father. I won't let you down.
	The matchmaker is not a patient woman.
	I should have prayed to the ancestors for luck.
	To please your future in-laws, you must demonstrate a sense of dignity and refinement.
	I will serve the Emperor in my father's place.
	It is an honor to protect my country and my family.
	Go! The fate of the Fa family rests in your claws.
	It's going to take a miracle to get me into the army.
	You will assemble swiftly and silently every morning.
	You gave away our position!
	You gotta learn to let these things go.
	The flower that blooms in adversity is the most rare and beautiful of all.
	Your Majesty, the Huns have crossed our northern border.
	Impossible. No one can get through the Great Wall.
	Honorable ancestors, please help Mulan impress the matchmaker today.
	We are counting on you to uphold the family honour.
	What beautiful blossoms we have this year!

Section III English Chat Task

Direction: *Discuss the themes of this movie and organize your presentations on the specific themes* (*Table 1.4*).

Table 1.4   Themes of *Mulan* (1998)

Themes	Questions about Themes	Answers (Key Words for Each Question)
Love	• Why does Mulan leave home at night without anyone knowing? • What's your understanding of "love"?	
Courage	• Why was it a crime for a woman to enlist in the army? • How does Mulan take the fact that she failed to hide her true identity in the army?	
Responsibility	• Why is it important for Mulan and others in the movie not to shame their families? • Why do the ancestors care about what happens to Mulan?	
Loyalty	• How can a girl bring honours to her family? • Mulan's father gets the order to serve in the army to protect his country. How does he feel about it?	
Survival	• Does the emperor punish Mulan for what she has done? What does he do? • Think about the role of female in ancient China. What are the standards for a good daughter and a good wife?	

Section IV   EANLIC Party Tasks

☞ **1. Give a presentation on the theme of "Mulan's spirit"**

☞ **2. Role-play**

Direction: *Prepare this part in groups before class, and then do the role-play in class. Scan the QR code for role-play scripts.*

(1) Mulan's being late for the meeting with the matchmaker.
(2) The meeting doesn't go well as expected.
(3) The Fa family gets the emperor's order to serve in the army. Mulan's father is too old to join the army. Mulan decides to take her father's place. She leaves home at night …

3. Debate

Direction: *Study the debate information in Reference 2 of this unit, and then begin your debate with the given format.*

(1) Is *Mulan* primarily a story about gender equality or is it more centered on individual bravery?

For: *Mulan* is primarily a story about gender equality.

Against: *Mulan* is more centered on individual bravery.

(2) Is *Mulan* primarily a tale of cultural identity or is it more about national pride?

For: *Mulan* is primarily a tale of cultural identity.

Against: *Mulan* is more about national pride.

Section V After-class Tasks

1. Mindmap drawing

Direction: *Read Reference 1 of this unit once again, and then draw a mindmap of Mulan's journey with key words.*

2. Movie review

Direction: *Enjoy reading the following movie review sample of* Mulan *(1998). Scan the QR code for the movie review sample and addresses attached for your further study.*

References

1. Hero's journey

In *The Hero with a Thousand Faces*, Joseph Campbell, a professor of literature at Sarah Lawrence College, unpacks his theory that all mythological narratives share the same basic structure. He refers to this structure as the "hero's journey". Campbell summarizes it like this: "A hero ventures forth from the world of common day into a region of supernatural wonder: fabulous forces are there encountered and a decisive victory is won: the hero comes back from this mysterious adventure with the power to bestow boons on his fellow man." It is a common story structure for modeling both plot points and character development. A hero embarks on an adventure into the unknown. He learns lessons, overcomes adversity, defeats evil, and returns home transformed. The hero's journey can be boiled down to 12 stages as follows.

Stages of the hero's journey

Ordinary world
The hero's normal life at the start of the story, before the adventure begins.

Call to adventure
The hero faces a challenge or problem that makes him or her begin the adventure.

Refusal of the call
The hero refuses the journey because of fear and insecurities. However, they are eventually convinced to go.

Meeting the mentor
The hero meets the mentor who gives him advice, confidence, training or gifts to overcome the fear of the journey. The mentor is to prepare him for what lies ahead.

Crossing the threshold
With the mentor's help, the hero is committed to the journey and ready to step across the threshold into the special world with unfamiliar rules and values.

Trials and tests
The hero steps into the special world, learns the new rules of an unfamiliar setting and is tested in the new world.

Stages of the hero's journey

Approach to innermost cave

This is a time of preparation for major change. It is a lesson of persistence for the hero. The hero tries new ideas and changes his or her mindset.

The ordeal

This is usually the climax of the hero's journey. The hero meets crisis and confronts with his or her greatest fear.

The reward

The hero takes possession of the treasure won by facing death. The hero gets a special weapon, treasure, protective device, or new knowledge that will be useful on the journey.

The road back

The hero is driven to complete the adventure, leaving the special world to return home. The hero is not out of the woods yet.

The resurrection

By the hero's action, the evils that were in conflict at the beginning are finally resolved. The hero emerges from the special world, transformed by his/her experience.

Return with the elixir

The hero officially returns to his/her ordinary world. The hero brings back some sort of "elixir" that changes him or her and elevates the hero to a new status quo because of the journey.

☞ 2. What is a debate?

A debate speech is a formal and well-written argument that seeks to refute an opponent's claim while elaborating on your own. Debate may help you improve your critical thinking abilities, teamwork abilities, public speaking abilities, and persuasive abilities.

The main purpose of a debate speech is to convince the judges and audience that your opinion is right. In a debate speech, you need to express your views in a specific format and make your opponents impress by good debate writing skills. Similarly, it is also a persuasive manner of speaking to convert one's opinion into your viewpoint.

Following a proper structure and format in debates is essential for a good debater to convenience the audience. Structuring and organizing your debate properly will increase your chance of success. Here is an example of a debate format in the following mindmap.

Debate procedures

Introduction

For
- Good afternoon, ladies and gentlemen. The topic for our debate is "That …".
- We define the topic as …
- We the affirmative team believe that this statement is true.

Against
- Good afternoon, ladies and gentlemen. The topic for our debate is "That …".
- We agree with the definition given by the affirmative team or we disagree with the definition given by the opposition.
- However, we the negative team believe that this statement is false.

Team split

For
- Today as the first speaker, I will be talking to you about …
- Our second speaker will be talking about …
- Our third speaker will rebut and sum up our team case.

Against
- Today as the first speaker, I will be talking to you about …
- Our second speaker will be talking about …
- Our third speaker will rebut and sum up our team case.

Rebuttal

For

There is no rebuttal for the first affirmative speaker.

Against
- The first speaker of the affirmative team has tried to tell you … This is wrong because …
- She/He also said that … This is wrong because …

Arguments

For
- My first point/argument is … This is because … /The reason for this is … (Explain the reason that supports your point.)
- If you have some more points, continue to list them.
- Now to my second point/argument … This is because … (Share a reason that supports and explains your second point/argument.)
- If you have some more points, continue to list them.

Against
- I will be discussing … points. My first point/argument is … This is because/The reason for this is … (Explain the reason that supports your point/argument.)
- Now to my second point … This is because … (Explain the reason that supports your second point/argument.)
- If you have some more points, continue to list them.

Ending

For / Against

So Mr/Madam chairman, ladies and gentlemen, in conclusion, we … (Finish your debate with a sentence that sums up what your team believes. You can use humor or a quote or you may say "thank you" to finish.)

Unit 2

The Lion King 1

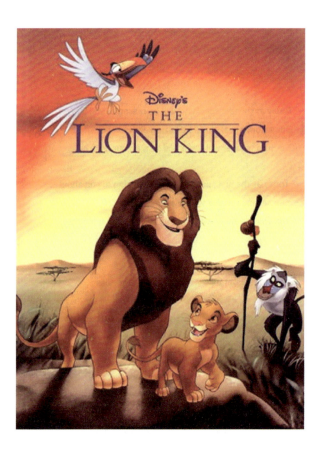

Unit Objectives:

1. Speaking skills:
   - Gain proficiency in retelling stories with the story spine structure.
   - Learn how to initiate a debate using a proper format.
2. Emotional objectives:
   - Cultivate students' courage to face challenging situations.
   - Foster a sense of responsibility towards their community and society.
   - Strengthen parent-child relationships.

Section I Pre-class Tasks

The students are supposed to watch the movie of *The Lion King 1* for at least 2 or 3 times ahead of the class, the first time for general understanding of the movie, and the second and third times for more detailed understanding and learning of English language, and then complete the following tasks before the class time.

☞ 1. Classic movie lines

Direction: *Read and recite the following lines from the movie.*
(1) Everything you see exists together in a delicate balance.
(2) You can't change the past. But I think you can either run from it or learn from it.
(3) This is my kingdom. If I don't fight for it, who will?

☞ 2. Background knowledge

Direction: *Go through the passage and prepare to share the information in class.*

The story is set in a kingdom of anthropomorphic animals in Africa known as Pride Lands, where a lion rules over other animals as king. Simba, son of King Mufasa and Queen Sarabi, heir to Pride Lands is presented to the animals of the kingdom.

Scar, Simba's uncle, Mufasa's brother, is absent from the ceremony, because he has always been plotting to be the King and the birth of Simba makes taking the throne harder.

Being tempted by Scar, Simba and his good friend Nala almost get killed at the elephant graveyard by the hyenas, who have made a deal with Scar to kill Simba. Seeing this plot fails, Scar devises another one: to kill Simba in an animal stampede with the help of the hyenas. Simba survives the stampede, but his father dies in order to save him. Scar misleads Simba about the cause of Mufasa's death. Simba runs away from Pride Lands because he is convicted that it is him who caused the death of Mufasa. He is saved by Timon and Pumbaa, and they live happily and freely together in the faith of "Hakuna Matata".

Scar takes the throne and begins his reign of Pride Lands. The kingdom declines under his rule.

Simba grows into a young adult lion. One day he meets Nala, who tells him about the declining of Pride Lands and how they wish Simba to be the King. The two lions fall in love with each other. With the help of Rafiki and Mufasa's ghost, Nala convinces Simba to return to Pride Lands and claim the throne. Simba, along with Nala, Timon, and Pumbaa, goes back to Pride Rock to confront Scar. Simba defeats Scar and takes the throne back. Scar gets killed by the hyenas, who find out Scar sells them out by telling Simba the truth about Mufasa's death.

Pride Lands turns green with life again and Rafiki presents Simba and Nala's newborn cub. A new circle of life begins.

👉 3. Vocabulary

Direction: *Learn these new words from this movie and try to use them in the EANLIC night.*

unwind /ʌnˈwaɪnd/ *v.* to reverse the winding or twisting of 放松发条,展开

hernia /ˈhɜːnɪə/ *n.* rupture in smooth muscle tissue through which a bodily structure protrudes 疝气

quiver /ˈkwɪvə(r)/ *v.* to shake with fast, tremulous movements 颤抖,发抖

impeccable /ɪmˈpekəbl/ *adj.* without fault or error 完美的,无缺点的

timing /ˈtaɪmɪŋ/ *n.* the act of choosing when when something happens 定时,时间的选择

mingle /ˈmɪŋgl/ *v.* to get involved or mixed-up with (使)混合

commoner /ˈkɒmənə(r)/ *n.* a person who holds no title 平民

slippery /ˈslɪpəri/ *adj.* causing or tending to cause things to slip or slide (因潮湿或有油脂而)滑的,滑溜的

curtsy /ˈkɜːtsi/ *n.* a gesture of respect made by women by bending the knees (女子)行屈膝礼

mangy /ˈmeɪndʒi/ *adj.* having many worn or threadbare spots in the nap 破旧的

savanna /səˈvænə/ *n.* flat grassland in tropical or subtropical regions (生态)热带草原

betrothed /bɪˈtrəʊðd/ *n.* the person to whom you are engaged 已订婚者

affiance /əˈfaɪəns/ *n.* 婚约;信托

creepy /ˈkriːpi/ *adj.* causing a sensation as of things crawling on your skin 诡异的,令人毛骨悚然的

stooge /stuːdʒ/ *n.* a person of unquestioning obedience 傀儡,走狗

stinky /ˈstɪŋki/ *adj.* having an unpleasant smell 难闻的,有臭味的

sordid /ˈsɔːdɪd/ *adj.* morally degraded 卑鄙的,龌龊的

outcast /ˈaʊtkɑːst/ *n.* a person who is rejected (from society or home) 被(家庭、社会等)遗弃(排斥)的人,被逐出者

exterior /ɪkˈstɪərɪə(r)/ *n.* the outer side or surface of something 外部,外观

adieu /əˈdjuː/ *n.* a farewell remark 道别,再见

brute /bruːt/ *n.* a cruelly rapacious person 畜生,残暴的人

hunch /hʌntʃ/ *n.* a feeling that sth. is true even though you do not have any evidence to prove it 预感,直觉

grunt /grʌnt/ *v.* to make a short low sound in your throat, especially to show that you are in pain, annoyed or not interested 发出哼声

snort /snɔːt/ *v.* to make a loud sound by breathing air out noisily through your nose, especially to show that you are angry or amused 喷鼻息,哼(尤其表示被惹恼或逗乐)

poacher /ˈpəʊtʃə(r)/ *n.* someone who hunts or fishes illegally on the property of another 偷猎

者,偷捕者

pathetic /pəˈθetɪk/ *adj.* deserving or inciting pity 招人怜悯的,可怜的

trespasser /ˈtrespəsə(r)/ *n.* someone who intrudes on the privacy or property of another without permission 非法侵入者,闯入者

navigational /ˌnævɪˈɡeɪʃnəl/ *adj.* of or relating to navigation 航行的,航运的

murk /mɜːk/ *adj.* dark or gloomy 阴暗的,黑暗的

tenacity /təˈnæsəti/ *n.* persistent determination 韧性

descend /dɪˈsend/ *v.* to move downward and lower, but not necessarily all the way 下来,下降

blossom /ˈblɒsəm/ *v.* to produce or yield flowers 开花

☞ 4. Character description

Direction: *Describe the main characters by using at least 5 adjectives in this movie with the reference of the words you have learned, and find examples in the movie to support your ideas (Table 2.1).*

Table 2.1 Main Characters in *The Lion King 1*

Main Characters	Adjectives	Examples
Mufasa		
Sarabi		
Simba		
Nala		
Scar		
Hyenas		
Timon & Pumbaa		

Section II In-class Tasks

☞ 1. Workshop

Direction: *Discuss the questions with your classmates, and use the following sentence structures if it is possible.*

Sentence structures

- *This movie reminds me of …*
- *This movie helps me … so that …*
- *This movie has changed me by …*
- *This movie stands out to me because …*
- *The movie suggests that the primary solution for a problem …*
- *The most important part about … is …*

(1) What do you like or dislike about *The Lion King 1*?

(2) How do you apply what you have learned from this movie into your life?

(3) How does Simba change as he grows up?

(4) Are Timon and Pumbaa just there for comic relief, or do they play a larger role?

(5) How are characters in *The Lion King 1* portrayed as good or evil?

(6) Who is your favourite character in this movie? Why?

(7) What's your understanding of "A strong man stands up for himself; a stronger man stands up for others"?

☞ 2. Cloze

Direction: *Fill in the gaps in the following passages taken from the movie with the words or phrases given below.*

■ **Passage 1**

circle	despair	take in	planet	seen	find
keeps	blinking	rolling high	unwinding	moves	place
hope	round	done	love	faith	

From the day we arrive on the ___1___. And ___2___, step into the sun. There's more to see than can ever be ___3___. More to do than can ever be ___4___. There's far too much to ___5___ here. More to ___6___ than can ever be found. But the sun ___7___, through the sapphire sky, ___8___ great and small on the endless ___9___. It's the circle of life. And it ___10___ us all, through ___11___ and ___12___, through ___13___ and ___14___, till we find our ___15___, on the path ___16___, in the ___17___ of life.

■ **Passage 2**

truth	peace	evening	living	holding	magic
bottom	romantic	perfect	things	falls	where
sweet	carefree	uncertainties	world		

I can see what's happening. What and they don't have a clue. Who, they'll fall in love and here's the ___1___ line. Our trio's down to two. The ___2___ caress of twilight. There's ___3___ everywhere. And with all this ___4___ atmosphere, disaster's in the air.

Can you feel the love tonight? The ___5___ the ___6___ brings. The ___7___ for once in ___8___ harmony, with all its ___9___ things. So many ___10___ to tell her, but how to make her see? The ___11___ about my past, impossible; she'd turn away from me. He's ___12___ back; he's hiding. But what, I can't decide. Why won't he be the king I know?

He is the king I see inside. Can you feel the love tonight? Can you feel the love tonight? You needn't look too far, stealing through the night's ___13___. Love is ___14___ they are. And if he ___15___ in love tonight, it can be assumed, his ___16___ days with us are history. In short, our pal is doomed.

☞ **3. Story retelling**

Direction: *Study the information in Reference 1 on the story spine structure of this unit, and then retell the story of "The Lion King 1" by using specific details to support your ideas (Table 2.2).*

Table 2.2 The Story Spine Structure about *The Lion King 1*

The Story Spine Structure		The Lion King 1
Beginning	Once upon a time …	
	Every day …	
The event	But, one day …	
Middle	Because of that …	
	Because of that …	
The climax	Until finally …	
End	And, ever since then …	

☞ **4. Sentence rearrangement**

Direction: *Put the following sentences into the chronological order based on the story of The Lion King 1 (Table 2.3).*

Table 2.3 Sentences from *The Lion King 1*

Orders	Sentences
	I'm only brave when I have to be. Being brave doesn't mean you go looking for trouble.
	I laugh in the face of danger.
	I'm here to announce that King Mufasa is on his way, so you'd better have a good excuse for missing the ceremony this morning.
	This is my kingdom. If I don't fight for it, who will?
	Everything you see exists together in a delicate balance.
	I was just trying to be brave like you!
	Somebody once told me that the great kings of the past are up there, watching over us.
	His carefree days with us are history.
	Simba, you must understand ... the pressures of ruling a kingdom.
	Look, Simba. Everything the light touches is our kingdom.
	I shall practice my curtsy.
	Didn't your mother ever tell you not to play with your food?
	I know what I have to do. But going back means I'll have to face my past. I've been running from it for so long.
	Don't turn your back on me.
	Temper, temper. I wouldn't dream of challenging you.
	It's the circle of life. And it moves us all, through despair and hope, through faith and love, till we find our place, on the path unwinding in the circle of life.

Section III English Chat Task

Direction: *Discuss the themes of this movie and organize your words on the specific themes (Table 2.4).*

Table 2.4 Themes of *The Lion King 1*

Themes	Questions about Themes	Answers (Key Words for Each Question)
Family	• What are the qualities of a good family in *The Lion King 1*? • How does the circle of life relate to the concept of family?	
Manipulation	• How does Scar manipulate other characters in *The Lion King 1*? • What happens as a result of Scar's manipulations?	
Principles	• What principles are parts of Simba's education? • What happens when the principles of the Pride Lands are abandoned?	
Good VS. Evil	• How does Simba come to understand who/what is good and who/what is evil? • What characteristics help us distinguish evil characters from good ones?	
Society and Class	• How are hyenas portrayed as different from or inferior to the other animals? • Do the hyenas benefit from Scar's new regime, where lions and hyenas are to live in harmony?	

Section IV EANLIC Party Tasks

☞ 1. Give a presentation on the theme of "Mufasa's spirit"

☞ 2. Role-play

Direction: *Prepare this part in groups before class, and then do the role-play in class. Scan the QR code for role-play scripts.*
　(1) The King teaches his son a lesson.
　(2) When Nala and Simba reunites in the forest.

3. Debate

Direction: *Study the debate information in Reference 2 of this unit, and then begin your debate with a proper format.*

(1) What really brings Simba back to Pride Rock is a sense of responsibility rather than a desire for power.

For: What really brings Simba back to Pride Rock is a sense of responsibility.

Against: What really brings Simba back to Pride Rock is just a desire for power.

(2) The ongoing battle between Scar and Mufasa is a battle between good and evil rather than one between two groups of people with different opinions.

For: The ongoing battle between Scar and Mufasa is a battle between good and evil.

Against: The ongoing battle between Scar and Mufasa is simply a common battle between two groups of people with different opinions.

Section V After-class Tasks

1. Draw a mindmap

Direction: *Read Reference 1 of this unit once again, and then draw a mindmap on the story of The Lion King 1.*

2. Movie review

Direction: *Enjoy reading the movie review sample in Unit 1. Scan the QR code for the movie review sample and addresses attached for your further study.*

References

1. The story spine structure

The story spine is a method both writers and performers use to make fascinating stories for audience, originally created by playwright Kenn Adams. The story spine helps with the structure of any movie, Broadway play or narrative. To them, this method is the basic foundation for any well-constructed story if they intend to use it to engage their audience. The following seven steps include an introduction that sets the stage for your protagonists, an occurrence that breaks their daily routine, a mid-point that shows the results of that change, a climax that builds up the story to a final resolution, and then an actual resolution which one hopes is a happy ending. To find the spine of a story, identify what the protagonists desire and what is the obstacle in their way that prevents them from achieving their goal. Study their emotions and how they change and the story progresses as the character gains hope.

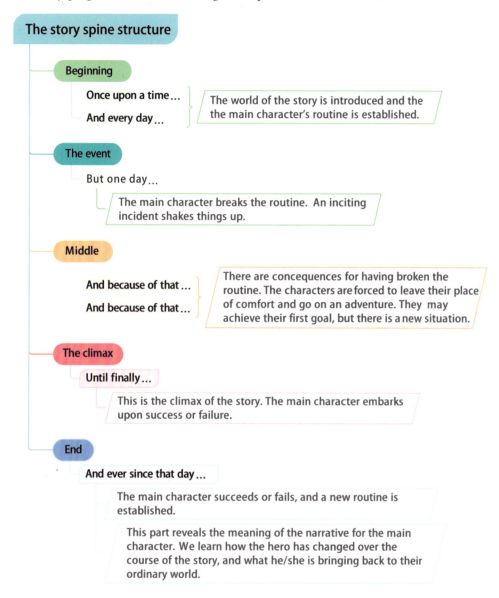

☞ 2. How to organize a debate?

A debate is meant to be an open discussion about a topic, usually viewing the topic at hand either being negative or positive. You can learn the details on how to organize a debate from the following mindmap.

How to organize a debate?

Know who is participating

- Knowing who is participating allows you to accurately plan and organize a debate.
- Be certain not to have too many participants, as this may lead to confusion and loudness.

Tell your participants to prepare

- Nothing is worse than having several people not knowing what they are talking about.
- Tell your participants to write some key points they would like to discuss.

Have a method to the madness

- Have a spokesperson for each side to speak on behalf of their respective side of the debate.
- Ensure that not only one person leads each side of the debate. Allow people on each side to switch out every five to ten minutes.

Do not allow it to go on and on

- Do not allow your debate to veer off track completely. As an organizer, you should defeat the purpose of the debate and strive for the best results a debate can have.

Find a pleasant solution

- A debate should reach an end when both sides reach a conclusion or present all of their opinions and facts.
- A solution will not always be found, but a compromise or general understanding should mark the end of a debate.

Create an artificial ending

- Ask for a vote from the general assembly of people on both inputs of the debate groups. If the debate is still split, consider reorganizing at a later date and finishing on a more defined ground.

Maintain a respective and neutral environment

- Do not allow participants (or if applicable audiences) to interrupt your debate.

Unit 3 　Kung Fu Panda 1

Unit Objectives:

1. Speaking skills:
   - Acquire the ability to tell a story with proper narration techniques.
   - Learn the appropriate method for starting a debate using the "debate speech structure".
2. Emotional objectives:
   - Encourage and cultivate a sense of persistence for achieving dreams in students.
   - Foster a sense of perseverance towards accomplishing long-term goals.
   - Encourage and motivate students to continue pushing forward even in the face of adversity.

Section I Pre-class Tasks

The students are supposed to watch the movie of *Kung Fu Panda 1* for at least 2 or 3 times ahead of the class, the first time for general understanding of the movie, and the second and third times for more detailed understanding and learning of English language, and then complete the following tasks before the class time.

☞ 1. Classic movie lines

Direction: *Read and recite the following lines from the movie.*
(1) There is a saying: Yesterday is history. Tomorrow is a mystery. But today is a gift. That is why it's called the present (the gift).
(2) You cannot leave. Real warrior never quits.
(3) To make something special, you just have to believe it's special.

☞ 2. Background knowledge

Direction: *Go through the passage and prepare to share the information in class.*

The film centers on Po, who is a big, enthusiastic and clumsy panda working in his family's noodle shop. Day after day, he works in the noodle shop in the valley dreaming. He is a big fan of kung fu and dreams of being a kung fu master. One day, he is unexpectedly selected to fulfill an ancient prophecy.

Po studies kung fu together with his idols—the Furious Five, Tigress, Crane, Mantis, Viper and Monkey, under the guidance of Master Shifu. He is supposed to defeat Tai Lung, the vengeful and treacherous snow leopard and restore peace to the valley. Po puts his heart and his girth into the task and the unlikely hero ultimately finds that his greatest weaknesses turn out to be his greatest strengths. He realizes his dream of being a kung fu master.

☞ 3. Vocabulary

Direction: *Learn these new words from this movie and try to use them at EANLIC night.*

awesome /ˈɔːsəm/ *adj.* very impressive or very difficult and perhaps rather and often frightening 让人惊叹的,令人敬畏的,使人畏怯的
mantis /ˈmæntɪs/ *n.* predacious long-bodied large-eyed insect of warm regions; rests with forelimbs raised as in prayer 螳螂
crane /kreɪn/ *n.* a kind of large bird with a long neck and long legs 鹤
viper /ˈvaɪpə(r)/ *n.* a small poisonous snake found mainly in Europe 毒蛇,蝰蛇
ferocity /fəˈrɒsəti/ *n.* the ferocity of something is its fierce or violent nature 凶猛残暴,暴行
subtlety /ˈsʌtlti/ *n.* the small but important details or aspects of sth. 微妙,细微差别

summon /ˈsʌmən/ *v.* to officially order someone to come to a meeting, a court of law 召唤, 传唤

agitated /ˈædʒɪteɪtɪd/ *adj.* showing in your behavior that you are anxious and nervous 不安的

tournament /ˈtʊənəmənt/ *n.* a sports competition in which players who win a match continue to play further matches in the competition until just one person or team is left 锦标赛

blade /bleɪd/ *n.* the edge of a knife, axe or saw, which is used for cutting 刀刃

flabby /ˈflæbi/ *adj.* having soft loose flesh（肌肉）松软的

crossbow /ˈkrɒsbəʊ/ *n.* a weapon consisting of a small, powerful bow that is fixed across a piece of wood, and aimed like a gun 弩, 十字弓

immobilize /ɪˈməʊbəlaɪz/ *v.* to stop them from moving or operating 使固定, 使停止

authentic /ɔːˈθentɪk/ *adj.* done or made in the traditional or original way 正宗的, 真正的

rhino /ˈraɪnəʊ/ *n.* a large heavy African or Asian animal with thick skin and either one or two horns on its nose 犀牛

destiny /ˈdestəni/ *n.* the things that will happen to someone in the future, especially those that cannot be changed or controlled 命运, 定数

trampoline /ˈtræmpəliːn/ *n.* a piece of equipment on which you jump up and down as a sport. It consists of a large piece of strong cloth held by springs in a frame 蹦床

hygiene /ˈhaɪdʒiːn/ *n.* the practice of keeping yourself and your surroundings clean, especially in order to prevent illness or the spread of diseases 卫生

ridiculous /rɪˈdɪkjələs/ *adj.* silly or unreasonable 滑稽的

pinky /ˈpɪŋki/ *n.* the smallest finger of the human hand 小手指

nauseous /ˈnɔːziəs/ *adj.* feeling as if you want to vomit 令人作呕的

bicep /baɪˈsep/ *n.* the large muscle on the front of your upper arm 二头肌

outnumber /ˌaʊtˈnʌmbə(r)/ *v.* to be more in number than another group 数量上超过

awkward /ˈɔːkwəd/ *adj.* making you feel so embarrassed that you are not sure what to do or say 尴尬的, 为难的

archer /ˈɑːtʃə(r)/ *n.* someone who shoots arrows using a bow 弓箭手

resume /rɪˈzjuːm/ *v.* to start doing something again after a pause or interruption 继续

combat /ˈkɒmbæt/ *n.* organized fighting, especially in a war 格斗, 战斗

flexibility /ˌfleksəˈbɪləti/ *n.* the ability to bend or be bent easily 柔韧性

knuckle /ˈnʌkl/ *n.* the rounded pieces of bone that form lumps on your hands where your fingers join your hands, and where your fingers bend 指节

bounce /baʊns/ *n.* the action of moving up and down on a surface 弹跳

acupuncture /ˈækjupʌŋktʃə(r)/ *n.* the treatment of a person's illness or pain by sticking small needles into their body at certain places 针灸

outrage /ˈaʊtreɪdʒ/ *v.* to make someone feel very angry and shocked 使愤慨, 使愤怒

☞ 4. Character description

Direction: *Describe the main characters by using at least 5 adjectives in this movie with the reference of the words you have learned, and find examples in the movie to support your ideas (Table 3.1).*

Table 3.1 Main Characters in *Kung Fu Panda 1*

Main Characters	Adjectives	Examples
Po		
Mr. Ping		
Master Shifu		
Tai Lung		
Monkey		
Crane		
Tigress		
Oogway		
Viper		
Mantis		

Section II In-class Tasks

☞ 1. Workshop

Direction: *Discuss the questions with your classmates, and use the following sentence structures if it is possible.*

Sentence structures

- First of all, I'd like to point out …
- The main problem is …
- The question of …
- Speaking of …
- What we have to decide is …

(1) What do you like or dislike about *Kung Fu Panda 1*?

(2) What is Po's dream?

(3) What difficulties does Po face on his road to be the "dragon warrior"?

(4) Which character do you like most, and why?

(5) How do you apply what you have learned from this movie into your life?
(6) What are the crucial elements that help Po realize his dream?
(7) What does Po do to make his dream become true?

☞ 2. Cultural elements

Direction: *Fill out the following table with the information you have learned from this movie (Table 3.2).*

Table 3.2　Traditional Chinese Elements in *Kung Fu Panda 1*

Chinese Elements	Examples
Regional landscape	Zhangjiajie, Qingcheng Mountain
Traditional Chinese architecture	Palace
Traditional Chinese stuff	
Chinese food	
Traditional Chinese music	
Traditional Chinese symbol	
Chinese philosophy	

☞ 3. Story retelling

Direction: *Study the following information in Reference 1 on narration of this unit, and then retell the story of* Kung Fu Panda 1 *by using specific details to support your ideas (Table 3.3).*

Table 3.3　Narrative Structure of *Kung Fu Panda 1*

Narrative Structure	*Kung Fu Panda 1*
Start or presentation: Also called balance situation or initial situation, it is the starting point of the story, in which the characters are introduced to us and their situation is detailed at the beginning of the plot.	**Start or presentation:**
Medium or complication: The characters are led to one or several situations of complexity, which threatens the satisfaction or dissatisfaction of their desires, and which rethinks the initial schemes in which each character was found.	**Medium or complication:**

continued

Narrative Structure	Kung Fu Panda 1
End or denouement: Final part in which conflicts are resolved in one way or another, for the good or bad of the characters, and they find themselves in a new balance situation.	**End or denouement**:

☞ 4. Sentence rearrangement

Direction: *Put the following sentences into the chronological order based on the story of Kung Fu Panda 1 (Table 3.4).*

Table 3.4 Sentences from *Kung Fu Panda 1*

Orders	Sentences
	Your mind is like this water, my friend. When it is agitated, it becomes difficult to see, but if you allow it to settle, the answer becomes clear.
	You don't know how long I've been waiting for this moment.
	Whomever I choose will not only bring peace to the valley but also to you.
	My patience is wearing thin.
	There is a saying: Yesterday is history. Tomorrow is a mystery. But today is a gift. That is why it's called the present (the gift).
	The true path to victory is to find your opponent's weakness and make him suffer for it.
	You must continue your journey without me.
	All we can do is resume our training and trust that in time the true Dragon Warrior will be revealed.
	You cannot leave. Real warrior never quits.
	The secret ingredient of my secret ingredient soup is ... nothing.
	It is said that dragon warrior can survive for months on nothing but the dew of ginkgo leaf and the energy of the universe.
	I will finally have paid for my mistake.
	Enough talk! Let's fight!

continued

Orders	Sentences
	Why didn't you quit? You know I was trying to get rid of you, but you stayed.
	To make something special, you just have to believe it's special.

Section III English Chat Task

Direction: *Discuss the themes of this movie and organize your words on the specific themes (Table 3.5).*

Table 3.5 Themes of *Kung Fu Panda 1*

Themes	Questions about Themes	Answers (Key Words for Each Question)
Parenting	• How do you think of Mr. Ping's parenting style? • Do you like his parenting style, why or why not?	
Collectivism	• How is collectivism reflected in the movie?	
Individualism	• How is individualism reflected in the movie?	
Adventure	• How does Po defeat Tai Lung? • How does Po become kung fu master?	
Dream	• How does Po fulfill his dream?	

Section IV EANLIC Party Tasks

☞ **1. Give a presentation on the theme of "Po's spirit"**

☞ **2. Role-play**

Direction: *Prepare this part in groups before class, and then do the role-play in class. Scan the QR code for role-play scripts.*

(1) The dream is over, and Po gets up to work.

(2) Master and his students are playing kung fu, and the bad news comes.

3. Debate

Direction: *Study the debate information in Reference 2 of this unit, and then begin your debate with the "debate speech structure".*

(1) Is inner strength and self-belief more important than natural talent in achieving success?

For: Inner strength and self-belief is more important in achieving success.

Against: Natural talent is more important in achieving success.

(2) Does *Kung Fu Panda* primarily teach us the importance of embracing our own uniqueness or does it emphasize the value of accepting and learning from others?

For: *Kung Fu Panda* primarily teaches us the importance of embracing our own uniqueness.

Against: *Kung Fu Panda* primarily emphasizes the value of accepting and learning from others.

Section V After-class Tasks

1. Mindmap drawing

Direction: *Read Reference 1 of this unit once again, and then draw a mindmap on the story of Kung Fu Panda 1.*

2. Movie review

Direction: *Enjoy reading the movie review sample in Unit 1. Scan the QR code for the movie review sample and addresses attached for your further study.*

References

1. What is narration?

Learning how to tell a good story is important. Storytelling is one of our most valuable assets in connecting with others. The power of stories is capable of moving people to action far better than any threat or incentive you can throw their way. Stories can relay important morals and lessons to students or listeners.

Narration means telling a series of events in an orderly, logical and sequential way, which builds a total unity when it nears its end and that, has a sense of causality and plausibility, which is credible and makes sense. In that sense, its structure traditionally involves three parts.

Narration

Elements

- **Characters:** protagonist (on whom the story focuses), antagonist (who opposes the protagonist), companion (who accompanies the protagonist).
- **Place:** Every story occurs in a real or imaginary place.
- **Time:** Every story involves an amount of time of the story's total duration (narrative time), as well as an amount of time elapsed between the events it narrates (story time).
- **Plot:** The content of the story itself, that is, the amount of actions that take place and that move the story towards its resolution and outcome.

Structure

- **Start or presentation:** It is the starting point of the story, also called balance situation or initial situation, in which the characters are introduced to us and their situation is detailed at the beginning of the plot.
- **Medium or complication:** The characters are led to one or several situations of complexity which threaten the satisfaction or dissatisfaction of their desires, and which rethink the initial schemes in which each character was found.
- **End or denouement:** It is the final part in which conflicts are resolved in one way or another, for the good or bad of the characters, and they find themselves in a new balance situation.

☞ **2. The debate speech structure**

The debate speech structure

- **Introduce yourself & Your position**

- **Argument topic 1**
- **Argument topic 2**

  Phrases for opinions
  - I think …
  - In my opinion …
  - As far as I'm concerned …
  - I'm convinced that …
  - I strongly believe that …

- **Rebuttal to opposing argument**

  Phrases for disagreeing
  - I don't think that …
  - I don't agree. I'd prefer …
  - Shouldn't we consider …
  - I'm afraid I don't agree …
  - The problem with your point of view is that …

- **Closing statement**

Unit 4

Brother Bear 1

Unit Objectives:

1. Speaking skills:
   - Develop the skills to effectively narrate a story using the SWBST format.
   - Understand how to begin a debate with a clear and well-organized outline.

2. Emotional objectives:
   - Cultivate a sense of love, empathy and appreciation for animals and nature in students.
   - Develop students' perspective-taking abilities, enabling them to consider from the viewpoints of others.
   - Foster a sense of co-existence between humans and the nature, emphasizing the importance of living in harmony with our environment.

Section I Pre-class Tasks

The students are supposed to watch the movie of *Brother Bear 1* for at least 2 or 3 times ahead of class, the first time for general understanding of the movie, and the second and third times for more detailed understanding and learning of English language, and then complete the following tasks before the class time.

☞ 1. Classic movie lines

Direction: *Read and recite the following lines from the movie.*

(1) Man and nature lived side by side.

(2) Love is the most precious of totems. It reveals itself in unexpected ways.

(3) You are going to get a whole new perspective on things.

☞ 2. Background knowledge

Direction: *Go through the passage and prepare to share the information in class.*

The film is set in a post-ice age Alaska, where the local tribesmen believe all creatures are created by the Spirits, who are said to appear in the form of an aurora. The Spirits have the power to change things.

Upon entering one's manhood, a man will receive a totem in the shape of a necklace from the shaman. Each totem presents a certain animal. The totem will guide a boy to grow into a man. Three brothers (Kenai, the youngest brother; Denahi, the middle brother; and Sitka, the eldest brother) live together. Sitka's totem is eagle (symbolizing guidance), Denahi a wolf (symbolizing wisdom) and Kenai receives a totem of bear (symbolizing love). Kenai thinks love has nothing to do with being a man, so he doesn't quite like his totem. A bear steals the salmons from Kenai, and Sitka dies in order to save his brothers while pursing the bear trying to get the fish back, which makes Kenai dislike bears more. Kenai kills the bear to avenge Sitka, but he is transformed into a bear by Sitka's spirit. Denahi misunderstands what happens to Kenai, and decides to kill the bear to avenge Kenai.

Kenai takes the advice of Tanana, the shaman of the tribe to go to the mountain, find Sitka and be transformed to be a human being again. He meets Koda who happens to help him get out of a trap. They form a sibling-like attachment. Once while listening to Koda telling a story about his mother fighting human hunters, Kenai learns the fact that it is him who kills Koda's mother. Although feeling guilty about what he has done, Kenai reveals the truth to Koda, who runs away with grief. At this time, Denahi arrives to confront Kenai. Koda comes back to help Kenai. Sitka's spirit appears and transforms Kenai into a man. But out of love, Kenai asks Sitka to turn him back to a bear for Koda needs him. Kenai grows into a real man through being a bear. His totem the bear of love guides him to become a man.

☞ 3. Vocabulary

Direction: *Learn these new words and expression(s) from this movie and try to use them at EANLIC night.*

roam /rəʊm/   *v.* to walk or travel, usually for a long time, with no clear purpose or direction 闲逛,漫步

shaman /ˈʃeɪmən/   *n.* a person in some tribes who is a religious leader and is believed to be able to talk to spirits and cure illnesses 萨满教巫师

caribou /ˈkærɪbuː/   *n.* a North American reindeer 北美驯鹿

totem /ˈtəʊtəm/   *n.* an animal, plant, etc. that is thought to have a special spiritual connection with a particular tribe, especially in North America, or a figure made to look like the animal, etc. 图腾,图腾形象

bonehead /ˈbəʊnhed/   *n.* (*informal*) a stupid person 笨蛋,傻瓜

bump /bʌmp/   *n.* an area of skin that is raised because you have hit it on something (撞击造成的)肿块

perspective /pəˈspektɪv/   *n.* a way of thinking about something, especially one which is influenced by the type of person you are or by your experiences (思考问题的)角度,观点,想法

gull /ɡʌl/   *n.* a large common black and white seabird that lives near the sea 海鸥

crusty /ˈkrʌsti/   *adj.* (*informal*) bad-tempered 爱发脾气的,暴躁的

twig /twɪɡ/   *n.* a small very thin stem of wood that grows from a branch on a tree (树枝上的)细枝,嫩枝

beaver /ˈbiːvə(r)/   *n.* a North American animal that has thick fur and a wide flat tail, and cuts down trees with its teeth 河狸,海狸

moose /muːs/   *n.* a large brown animal like a deer that has very large flat antlers (＝horns that grow like branches) and lives in North America, northern Europe, and parts of Asia 驼鹿(产于北美、欧洲北部及亚洲部分地区)

swollen /ˈswəʊlən/   *adj.* larger than normal, especially as a result of a disease or an injury (身体部位)肿起的,肿胀的

salmon /ˈsæmən/   *n.* a large fish with silver skin and pink flesh that lives in the sea but swims up rivers to lay its eggs 鲑鱼,三文鱼,大麻哈鱼

cuddly /ˈkʌdli/   *adj.* a person or animal that is cuddly makes you want to cuddle them 可爱的,令人想拥抱的

ditch /dɪtʃ/   *v.* (*informal*) to stop having something because you no longer want it 扔掉,抛弃,丢弃

cramp /kræmp/   *n.* a severe pain that you get in part of your body when a muscle becomes too tight, making it difficult for you to move that part of your body 痛性痉挛,痉挛,抽筋

tadpole /ˈtædpəʊl/ *n.* a small creature that has a long tail, lives in water, and grows into a frog or toad 蝌蚪

vertical /ˈvɜːtɪkl/ *adj.* pointing up in a line that forms an angle of 90 with a flat surface 垂直的,直立的

pinecone /ˈpaɪnkəʊn/ *n.* one of the brown oval seed cases produced by a pine tree 松果

hibernate /ˈhaɪbəneɪt/ *v.* to sleep for the whole winter (动物)冬眠

depart /dɪˈpɑːt/ *v.* to leave, especially when you are starting a journey 离开(尤指动身去旅行),起程,上路

chipmunk /ˈtʃɪpmʌŋk/ *n.* a small American animal similar to a squirrel with black lines on its fur 花鼠,金花鼠,花栗鼠(产于美洲,皮毛上有黑色条纹)

cub /kʌb/ *n.* the baby of a wild animal such as a lion or a bear (狮、熊等的)幼兽

trample /ˈtræmpl/ *v.* to step heavily on something so that you crush it with your feet 踩,践踏

reckless /ˈrekləs/ *adj.* not caring or worrying about the possible bad or dangerous results of your actions 轻率的,鲁莽的,不顾后果的

salutation /ˌsæljuˈteɪʃn/ *n.* something you say or do when greeting someone 问候,致意

life-and-death *adj.* [only before noun] extremely serious, especially when there is a situation in which people might die 生死攸关的

Expression(s)

knock it off [美国俚语](用以喝止别人)住嘴,别说了;住手;别闹了
manhood ceremony 成年礼
chew off 嚼断
pinky swear 勾小指,拉钩

☞ 4. Character description

Direction: *Describe the main characters by using at least 5 adjectives in this movie with the reference of the words you have learned, and find examples in the movie to support your ideas (Table 4.1).*

Table 4.1 Main Characters in *Brother Bear 1*

Main Characters	Adjectives	Examples
Kenai		
Sitka		
Denahi		
Koda		

continued

Main Characters	Adjectives	Examples
Tanana		
Koda's mother		

Section II In-class Tasks

☞ 1. Workshop

Direction: *Discuss the questions with your classmates, and use the following sentence structures if it is possible.*

Sentence structures for expressing a personal opinion
- It seems to me that ...
- I'm absolutely convinced that ...
- Well, if you ask me ...
- The way I see it ...
- Personally, I believe/suppose/feel (that) ...

(1) Who are the major characters in the movie? What do you think about each main character?

(2) What are the totems for each of them: Kenai, Denahi, Sitka?

(3) What's your understanding of the relationship between human beings and the nature?

(4) Have you ever heard of the sentence "You never understand someone till you walk a mile in their shoes"? How do you think this sentence fits in with this story? Do you think Kenai truly began to understand the bears?

(5) Kenai feels like he has to get revenge on the bear for stealing his basket of fish. Is his response to the bear's theft fair? What would been a fair response? Have you ever reacted poorly to someone harming you in some way?

(6) Kenai becomes a man as a result of the totem ceremony. Are there any ceremonies or birthdays in your culture that represent your "coming-of-age" or "becoming growing up"? What do you think are important birthdays and why?

☞ 2. Cloze

Direction: *Fill in the gaps in the following passages taken from the movie with the words or phrases given below.*

Passage 1

man	ancestors	ever-changing	taught	roamed
shaman	magic	dance	changes	story
power	turns	source	desperately	spirits

This is a ___1___ from long ago, when the great mammoths still ___2___ our Lands. It's the story of my two brothers and me. When the three of us were young, we were ___3___ that the world is full of ___4___. The ___5___ of this magic is the ___6___ lights that ___7___ across the sky. The ___8___ woman of our village told us that these lights are the ___9___ of our ___10___ and that they have the ___11___ to make changes in our world. Small things become big. Winter ___12___ to spring. One thing always ___13___ into another. But the greatest change I ever saw was that of my brother, a boy who ___14___ wanted to be a ___15___.

Passage 2

wisdom	side by side	guidance	lead	wilderness	corner
young	kissed	spirits	strength	sweet	choices
wonder	joy	direction	same	journey	

When the earth was ___1___ and the air was ___2___, and the mountains ___3___ the sky, and the great beyond ... with its many paths, man and nature lived ___4___. In this ___5___ of danger and beauty, lived three brothers bonded by love. Their hearts full of ___6___. They ask now for ___7___, reaching out to the skies up above. Great ___8___ of all who lived before ... take our hands and ___9___ us, fill our hearts and souls with all you know, show us that in your eyes ... we are all the ___10___, brothers to each other in this world, we remain. Truly brothers, all the same. Give us ___11___ to pass to each other. And give us ___12___ so we understand. That the things we do, the ___13___ we make, give ___14___ to all life's plans. To look at ___15___ at all we've been given in a world that's not always as it seems. Every ___16___ we turn only leads to another. A ___17___ ends but another begins.

☞ **3. Story retelling**

Direction: *Study the information in Reference 1 on SWBST of this unit, and then retell the story of* Brother Bear 1 *by using specific details to support your ideas* (Table 4.2).

Table 4.2   SWBST in *Brother Bear 1*

SWBST Structure	Brother Bear 1
Somebody (Who are the main characters?)	
Wanted (What did the characters want?)	
But (What was the problem?)	
So (How did the main characters solve the problem?)	
Then (What was the resolution to the story? How did the story end?)	

☞ **4. Sentence rearrangement**

Direction：*Put the following sentences into the chronological order based on the story of Brother Bear 1 (Table 4.3).*

Table 4.3   Sentences from *Brother Bear 1*

Orders	Sentences
	Small things become big. Winter turns to spring. One thing always changes into another, but the greatest change I ever saw was that of my brother.
	This is a story from long ago.
	Man and nature lived side by side.
	We were taught that the world is full of magic.
	In this wilderness of danger and beauty lived three brothers bonded by love.
	I promise to help you escape from every trap you walk into.
	A man wouldn't just sit here and do nothing.
	When the Earth was young and the air was sweet, and the mountains kissed the sky ...
	You trust me, believe in me and I let you down.
	The quicker we get these fish, the faster we get to your ceremony.
	The shaman woman of our village told us that these lights are the spirits of our ancestors, and that they have the power to make changes in our world.

Orders	Sentences
	If only Edgar was alive.
	My eyes were watering and my tongue was swollen.
	Of all the things I hid from you, I cannot hide the shame.
	You are going to get a whole new perspective on things.

Section III English Chat Task

Direction: *Discuss the themes of this movie and organize your words on the specific themes (Table 4.4).*

Table 4.4 Themes of *Brother Bear 1*

Themes	Questions about Themes	Answers (Key Words for Each Question)
Love	• What is love? What is your understanding of love? • How do you understand "Love is powerful"?	
Friendship	• What is your understanding of "A friend in need is a friend indeed"? • What are the features of true friendship?	
Responsibility	• What does responsibility mean to you? • What are the main characters' responsibilities in this movie?	
Put yourself in others' shoes	• What's your understanding of this phrase? • How do you apply this into your own life?	
Survival	• How do you understand this saying "Natural selection, survival of the fittest"? • In what aspects has this movies proved this saying?	
Maturity	• What are the features of maturity? • What is your understanding of maturity?	

Section IV EANLIC Party Tasks

☞ 1. Give a presentation on the theme of *Brother Bear 1*

☞ 2. Role-play

Direction: Prepare this part in groups before class, and then do the role-play in class. Scan the QR code for role-play scripts.

（1）People gather together and Tanana reveals Kenai's totem to him.

（2）Kenai asks Denahi to go after the bear with him, but Denahi refuses.

（3）Kenai gets out of the trap with Koda's help, and he promises Koda to go to the salmon run together.

☞ 3. Debate

Direction: Study the debate information in Reference 2 of this unit, and then begin your debate with a clear and well-organized outline.

（1）Should humans be held accountable for the consequences of their actions on the environment and wildlife?

For: Humans should be held accountable for the consequences of their actions on the environment and wildlife.

Against: Humans don't have to be held accountable for the consequences of their actions on the environment and wildlife.

（2）Is it realistic to expect humans to live in harmony with the nature and wildlife?

For: It is realistic to expect humans to live in harmony with the nature and wildlife.

Against: It isn't realistic to expect humans to live in harmony with the nature and wildlife.

Section V After-class Tasks

☞ 1. Mindmap drawing

Direction: Read Reference 1 of this unit once again, and then draw a mindmap on the story of *Brother Bear 1*.

☞ 2. Movie review

Direction: Enjoy reading the movie review sample in Unit 1. Scan the QR code for the movie review sample and addresses attached for your further study.

References

☞ 1. What is SWBST?

Another strategy for recounting and retelling stories is the SWBST or "Somebody Wanted But So Then" format. The "Somebody-Wanted-But-So-Then" strategy is used during or after reading. It provides a framework to use when summarizing the action of a story or historical event by identifying key elements. The strategy also helps students identify the main ideas, recognize cause and effect relationships, make generalizations, identify differences between characters and look at various points of view. It is more often used with narrative stories.

A simple way to implement this strategy is to use it when you are reading or watching a movie. At the end of your reading or watching, stop and use the SWBST format to help you organize your story with the following information.

SWBST format

SWBST meaning
- S—Somebody: Who are the main characters?
- W—Wanted: What did the main characters want?
- B—But: What was the problem? What kept the main characters from getting what they wanted?
- S—So: How did the main characters solve the problem?
- T—Then: What was the resolution to the story? How did the story end?

Implement
- S—Somebody. Who was our story about?
- W—Wanted. What did they want in our story?
- B—But. What was the problem? Why couldn't they _____?
- S—So. What did they do to solve this problem?
- T—Then. How did the story end? What was the resolution?

characters

☞ 2. How to write a debate outline?

Although you may feel like you debate people all the time, writing a debate outline requires a bit more research and organization than simply arguing with someone. Fortunately, once you know how to effectively categorize and present the evidence for your argument, writing a debate outline is a relatively straightforward process.

How to write a debate outline?

- **Plan your outline**
  - Narrow down your topic.
  - Identify the purpose of your outline (inform, entertain or reflect).
  - Assemble your notes, research or supporting materials.
  - Identify your arguments or main ideas by brainstorming.
  - Develop a thesis or controlling idea for your outline.

- **Organize your ideas**
  - Group your ideas together.
  - Put each group in order (from broad ideas to specific details).
  - Outline your introduction as the first main point for a speech. Points you need in your introduction:
    - 1-2 hooks to grab the audience.
    - 1-2 general statements about your topic.
    - 1 thesis.
  - Write at least 2 sub-points for each main idea.
  - Add at least 2 supporting details for each sub-point:
    - Restate your thesis.
    - 1-2 summarizing sentences.
    - Write a concluding statement.

- **Finalize your outline**
  - Read over your outline to make sure you've achieved your purpose.
  - Revise your outline if ideas are missing or not fleshed out.

Unit 5

Ice Age 1

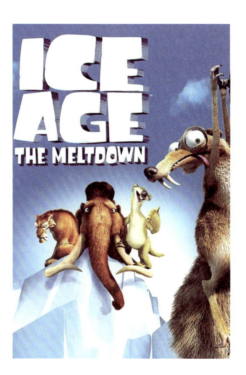

Unit Objectives:

1. Speaking skills:
   - Develop the skills to convincingly retell a story using persuasive techniques.
   - Understand how to effectively prepare for a debate, including gathering relevant reference information.

2. Emotional objectives:
   - Cultivate a sense of teamwork among students, encouraging cooperation and collaboration.
   - Foster a love for respecting and appreciating the nature, emphasizing the importance of preserving our environment.
   - Develop a sense of responsibility for environmental protection, highlighting the need for sustainable practices and conservation efforts.

Section I Pre-class Tasks

The students are supposed to watch the movie of *Ice Age 1* for at least 2 or 3 times ahead of the class, the first time for general understanding of the movie, and the second and third times for more detailed understanding and learning of English language, and then complete the following tasks before the class time.

☞ 1. Classic movie lines

Direction: *Read and recite the following lines from the movie.*
(1) Natural selection and survival of the fittest.
(2) Stay close. We can fight our way out.
(3) I gotta save whatever dignity I've got left.

☞ 2. Background knowledge

Direction: *Go through the passage and prepare to share the information in class.*

The film is set in a prehistoric ice age. Large herds of animals are migrating to the warmer south to avoid the cold in the north. Being abandoned by his family, Sid, a funny and clumsy ground sloth has to move to south all by himself. He meets Manny (Manfred), a mammoth heading north, who happens to save him from two rhinos. Not wanting to be alone and unprotected, Sid follows Manny.

A group of saber-toothed tigers leading by Soto attack a human tribe as a revenge for humans' killing of half of their pack. They plan to take the chief's baby son and eat him. The plan doesn't work out as expected, and the baby is lost. Diego, who is responsible of not catching the baby, is sent to find the baby and bring him back.

Sid and Manny finds the baby and his mother in the river. The baby survives and the mother disappears into the water. Sid is kind-hearted, and he seeks to persuade Manny into returning the baby to humans. When they arrive at the human settlement, they find them all gone. They meet Diego, who secretly plans to lead the three into a trap of saber-toothed tigers, persuades the two into allowing him to help return the baby. The four embark on their journey of returning the baby.

After many misadventures, the four eventually treat each other sincerely and return the baby to his father.

☞ 3. Vocabulary

Direction: *Learn these new words and expression(s) from this movie and try to use them at EANLIC night.*

chill /tʃɪl/ *n.* a feeling of coldness 寒冷,寒气
extinction /ɪkˈstɪŋkʃn/ *n.* when a particular type of animal or plant stops existing 灭绝,绝种

evolutionary /ˌiːvəˈluːʃənri/ *adj.* relating to the way in which plants and animals develop and change gradually over a long period of time 进化的

mammoth /ˈmæməθ/ *n.* an animal like a large hairy elephant that lived on Earth thousands of years ago 猛犸(象)，毛象

trunk /trʌŋk/ *n.* the very long nose of an elephant 象鼻

migration /maɪˈgreɪʃn/ *n.* the movement of large numbers of people, birds or animals travel regularly from one part of the world to another (鸟或兽的)迁徙

waddle /ˈwɒdl/ *v.* to walk with short steps, with your body moving from one side to another—used especially about people or birds with fat bodies and short legs (尤指体胖腿短的人或鸟) 摇摇摆摆地走

sloth /sləʊθ/ *n.* an animal in Central and South America that moves very slowly, has grey fur, and lives in trees 树懒

mammal /ˈmæml/ *n.* a type of animal that drinks milk from its mother's body when it is young 哺乳动物

dandelion /ˈdændɪlaɪən/ *n.* a wild plant with a bright yellow flower which later becomes a white ball of seeds that are blown away in the wind 蒲公英

hog /hɒg/ *v.* to keep, use, or have all of something that should be shared 攫取，把……占为己有，独占

impale /ɪmˈpeɪl/ *v.* to push a sharp pointed object through sth. (用尖物)刺穿，插进

bluff /blʌf/ *v.* to pretend something, especially in order to achieve what you want in a difficult or dangerous situation 虚张声势，吓唬，吹牛

bachelor /ˈbætʃələ(r)/ *n.* a man who has never been married 未婚男子，单身汉

shrewd /ʃruːd/ *adj.* well-judged and likely to be right 判断准确的，英明的

melancholy /ˈmelənkəli/ *n.* a feeling of sadness for no particular reason 忧郁，无名的伤感

brawn /brɔːn/ *n.* physical strength, especially when compared with intelligence 体力(尤与智力相对)

reptile /ˈreptaɪl/ *n.* a type of animal, such as a snake or lizard, whose body temperature changes according to the temperature around it, and that usually lays eggs to have babies 爬行动物

abandon /əˈbændən/ *v.* to leave someone, especially someone you are responsible for 抛弃，遗弃(某人)

blizzard /ˈblɪzəd/ *n.* a severe snowstorm 暴风雪

stinky /ˈstɪŋki/ *adj.* smelling unpleasant 难闻的，有臭味的

intruder /ɪnˈtruːdə(r)/ *n.* someone who illegally enters a building or area, usually in order to steal something 非法闯入者(通常指小偷)

retrieve /rɪˈtriːv/ *v.* to find something and bring it back 找回，收回，取回

infant /ˈɪnfənt/ *n.* a baby or very young child 婴儿，幼儿

snatch /snætʃ/　*v.* to take something away from someone with a quick, often violent movement 抢去,强夺,攫取

predator /ˈpredətə(r)/　*n.* an animal that kills and eats other animals 掠食动物,捕食性动物

thunder /ˈθʌndə(r)/　*n.* the loud noise that you hear during a storm, usually after a flash of lightning 雷声

lava /ˈlɑːvə/　*n.* hot liquid rock that flows from a volcano, or this type of rock when it has become solid (火山喷出的)岩浆,熔岩;火山岩

retreat /rɪˈtriːt/　*v.* to move away from the enemy after being defeated in battle 撤退

ambush /ˈæmbʊʃ/　*n.* a sudden attack on someone by people who have been hiding and waiting for them, or the place where this happens 伏击,埋伏;埋伏地点

revenge /rɪˈvendʒ/　*n.* something you do in order to punish someone who has harmed or offended you 报复,报仇

grudge /grʌdʒ/　*n.* a feeling of dislike for someone because you cannot forget that they harmed you in the past 怀恨,怨恨

Expression(s)

on the verge of　接近于……,濒于……
make a scene　(当众)大吵大闹,当众出丑
zip one's lip　不露风声,缄口不言

☞ 4. Character description

Direction:*Describe the main characters by using at least 5 adjectives in this movie with the reference of the words you have learned, and find examples in the movie to support your ideas (Table 5.1).*

Table 5.1　Main Characters in *Ice Age 1*

Main Characters	Adjectives	Examples
Sid		
Diego		
Manny		
Mammoths		
Rhinos		
Baby		

Section II In-class Tasks

☞ 1. Workshop

Direction: *Discuss the questions with your classmates, and use the following sentence structures if it is possible.*

Sentence structures for expressing pros and cons
- *There are two sides of the question.*
- *On the one hand …; on the other hand …*
- *An argument for/in favor of/against if …*
- *While admitting that … one should not forget that …*
- *Some people think that …, while others say that …*

(1) Why are the animals heading south?
(2) Why do the rhinos chase Sid?
(3) How does the baby get separated from his parents?
(4) Sid's family migrate without him this year. How did his family abandon him last year?
(5) Does Diego really want to return the baby? What's his real intention?
(6) What have mammoths been through according to the painting in the cave?
(7) Manny sees the painting on the wall in the cave. Does this make him hate the baby?
(8) Why does Manny save Diego?
(9) Manny risks his life to save Diego. What impact does it have on Diego?
(10) Diego tells Manny and Sid about the ambush awaiting them. Why does he do so?

☞ 2. Cloze

Direction: *Fill in the gaps in the following passage and dialogue taken from the movie with the words or phrases given below.*

■ Passage

gagged	tracks	asleep	abandoned	water
woke up	migrated	scent	mouse	tied

My family ___1___ me. They just kind of ___2___ without me. You should see what they did last year. They ___3___ early and ___4___ my hands and feet and they ___5___ me with a field ___6___, covered their ___7___, went through ___8___ so I'd lose their ___9___, and … who needs 'em, anyway? So what about you? You have family? OK, you're tired. I see. We'll talk more in the morning. Manfred? Manfred? Could you scorch over a drop? Come on. Nobody falls ___10___ that fast.

■ Dialogue

embarrassment	leave	return	gone	saved
smoke	up	get rid of	straight	mammoth
take care of	forgetting	cake	herd	

Sid: Look at that. He's OK.

　　　She's ___1___.

　　　Manny, are you ___2___ something?

Manfred: No.

Sid: But you just ___3___ him.

Manfred: I'm trying to ___4___ the last thing I saved.

Sid: But you can't ___5___ him here.

　　　Look! There's ___6___. That's his ___7___ right up the hill.

　　　We should ___8___ him.

Manfred: Let's get this ___9___. There is no "we".

　　　There never was a "we". In fact, without me, there wouldn't even be a "you".

Sid: Just ___10___ the hill.

Manfred: Listen very carefully: I'm not going.

Sid: Fine, be a jerk. I'll ___11___ him.

Manfred: Yeah, that's good.

　　　You can't even take care of yourself. This, I gotta see.

Sid: I'll return you. We don't need that meany-weeny ___12___, do we? No, we don't.

Manfred: You're an ___13___ to nature. Do you know that?

Sid: Piece of ___14___. I'm fine, I'm fine. I'm gonna die.

☞ 3. Story retelling

Direction: Study the information in Reference 1 on "persuasive techniques" of this unit, and then retell the story of *Ice Age 1* by using specific details to support your ideas (Table 5.2).

Table 5.2　Persuasive Techniques in *Ice Age 1*

Persuasive Techniques	Ice Age 1
Ask rhetorical questions	
Use personal anecdotes	
Use inclusive language	
Use emotive language	

☞ **4. Sentence rearrangement**

Direction: *Put the following sentences into the chronological order based on the story of* Ice Age 1 *(Table 5.3)*.

Table 5.3 Sentences from *Ice Age 1*

Orders	Sentences
	This has definitely not been my day. You know what I'm saying, buddy?
	Do the world a favor. Move your issues off the road.
	Don't let them impale me. I wanna live.
	So, you can give that baby to me, or go get lost in a blizzard. It's your choice.
	Stay close, Sid. We can fight our way out.
	The sooner we find the humans, the sooner I get rid of Mr. Stinky Drool-Face, and the baby, too.
	You know, Diego, I've never had a friend who would risk his life for me.
	Any of this A-ringing A bell?
	If my trunk was that small, I wouldn't draw attention to myself, pal.
	What a mess! You rhinos have tiny brains. Did you know that?

Section III English Chat Task

Direction: *Discuss the themes of this movie and organize your words on the specific themes (Table 5.4)*.

Table 5.4 Themes of *Ice Age 1*

Themes	Questions about Themes	Answers (Key Words for Each Question)
Determination	• What have you learned from the squirrel in this movie? • How would you apply what you have learned from it into your own life? • Does Manny also have strong determination to help the baby out? Please share your ideas with us.	

continued

Themes	Questions about Themes	Answers (Key Words for Each Question)
Friendship	• What is true friendship? What have you learned about friendship from the movie? • Can you think of some famous sayings about friendship?	
Righteousness	• What are the features of righteousness? • Can you think of any righteous characters in this movie? And what can you learn from them?	
Evil	• What is your understanding of evil? • Can you think of any evil characters in this movie? In what ways do they prove themselves as evil ones?	
Environment Protection	• What are the deadly natural disasters around the world in recent years? • What are the worst effects of those natural disasters? And what lessons did they want to teach human beings? • What can we do to protect the environment?	

Section IV   EANLIC Party Tasks

☞ 1. Give a presentation on the theme of *Ice Age 1*

☞ 2. Role-play

Direction: *Prepare this part in groups before class, and then do the role-play in class. Scan the QR code for role-play scripts.*

(1) Sid wakes up and finds that he's left alone.
(2) Sid goes south with Manny to avoid being confronted with the rhinos.
(3) The rhinos are chasing Sid, and Manfred helps Sid get away.

☞ 3. Debate

Direction: *Study the debate information in Reference 2 of this unit, and then prepare a debate with relevant information.*

(1) Should individuals prioritize personal survival or collective cooperation in times of crisis?

For: Individuals should prioritize personal survival in times of crisis.

Against: Individuals should prioritize collective cooperation in times of crisis.

(2) Is it morally justifiable to sacrifice personal comfort or safety for the sake of protecting the vulnerable?

For: It is morally justifiable to sacrifice personal comfort or safety for the sake of protecting the vulnerable.

Against: It isn't morally justifiable to sacrifice personal comfort or safety for the sake of protecting the vulnerable.

Section V After-class Tasks

☞ 1. Mindmap drawing

Direction: *Read Reference 1 of this unit once again, and then draw a mindmap on the story of* Ice Age 1.

☞ 2. Movie review

Direction: *Enjoy reading the movie review sample in Unit 1. Scan the QR code for the movie review sample and addresses attached for your further study.*

References

☞ 1. What are persuasive techniques?

Persuasive techniques are the methods or strategies that writers or speakers use to take a stance on an issue, convincing their readers or audience to agree with a certain idea or opinion. Writers or speakers vary their persuasive techniques based upon their audience, motives and writing genre.

Persuasive techniques play a crucial role in writing or story telling because they can help you get your point of view across more effectively. Whether you're writing or delivering an email to announce a new project, a proposal for a new approach to data collection or a user manual for an operating system, your aim is to convince your audience of the importance of what you're saying so that they respond positively to it. You will learn how to use the following persuasive techniques for speeches to convince your audiences.

Persuasive techniques

Ask rhetorical questions

- Force your audience to think. Rhetorical questions will get them to think about their own answers.
- Emphasize a specific point. This will make your audience think about the importance of what you said and agree with you.
- Evoke emotions. Rhetorical questions can evoke emotions by putting the audience in a situation where they can empathize with what is being discussed.

Use personal anecdotes

- Have a message. Select a story that supports your idea and hammers down your message by telling the audience what you learned at the end of your anecdote, for it helps you convince them to believe what you said.
- Use it with purpose. Ensure that you know exactly why you are using your anecdote to help you use it at the right time.
- Be descriptive. The audience wants to feel what you felt in your story. So, be descriptive and bring your story to life! Tell them what you thought!

Use inclusive language

- They are persuasive because they directly engage with your audience, and give them a sense of responsibility and inclusivity.
- "Us". Everyone loves to feel included. So, using first-person plural pronouns is a great way to engage your audience and extend your message to them.

Use emotive language

- It refers to the particular selection of words and phrases that appeal to the audience's emotions.
- Use adjectives and adverbs. It holds emotional weight to convince the audience.
- Use metaphors and similes. It compares one thing to another. This will help the audience imagine what you are describing and make your story sound more convincing.

☞ **2. How to prepare for a debate speech?**

A debate speech is a structured argument on a specific topic that is presented in a formal setting. The main purpose of a debate speech is to: express your point of view persuasively and effectively; convince the opposition that you are right; change the people's point of view on a particular topic. In a debate speech, the speaker presents his argument in a clear, concise, and convincing manner. Debate speeches have a set time limit, and the speaker must use his time effectively to make his case and address counterarguments. Therefore, you can only win your debate if you have spent time preparing it well. Follow the steps below to be prepared for your debate speech.

How to prepare for the debate speech?

Selecte a position

Choose a topic that you are passionate about. Once you have chosen a topic, narrow it down to a specific aspect that you can argue for or against. The clearer your position, the easier it will be to research and prepare your arguments.

Research and gather information

Research it thoroughly, once you have selected your topic. Gather as much information as you can from credible sources such as academic journals, news articles, and government reports.

Understand both sides of the argument

Consider the arguments that your opponents might make and anticipate counterarguments. This will help you to strengthen your own arguments and address potential weaknesses in your position.

Organize your arguments

Organize your arguments in a clear and logical way, once you have gathered all of the information you need.

Start by outlining the main points you want to make and then add supporting evidence to each point. Make sure that your arguments flow logically and build on each other.

Practice your delivery

Practise reading your speech out loud several times to get a feel for how it flows. Time yourself to make sure that you can fit all of your arguments into the allotted time.

Consider practising in front of a friend or family member to get feedback on your delivery.

Unit 6

Charlotte's Web

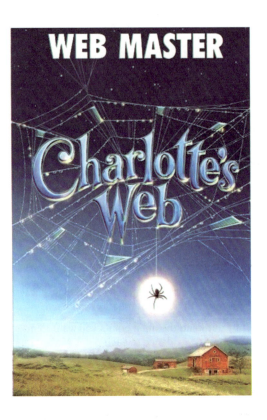

Unit Objectives:

1. Speaking skills:
   - Acquire the skills to retell the story from the movie with the SCQA format.
   - Learn effective methods for writing a persuasive debate speech.

2. Emotional objectives:
   - Cultivate a love and appreciation for animals, promoting empathy and compassion.
   - Develop a healthy perspective on friendship, encouraging students to value loyalty, honesty, and respect.
   - Foster a sense of inclusiveness, promoting a warm and welcoming classroom environment where everyone is included and valued.

Section I Pre-class Tasks

The students are supposed to watch the movie of *Charlotte's Web* for at least 2 or 3 times ahead of class, the first time for general understanding of the movie, and the second and third times for more detailed understanding and learning of English language, and then complete the following tasks before the class time.

☞ 1. Classic movie lines

Direction: *Read and recite the following lines from the movie.*

(1) Promises are something I never break.

(2) Good things come to those who wait.

(3) There's an old expression that says ignorance is bliss.

☞ 2. Background knowledge

Direction: *Go through the passage and prepare to share the information in class.*

A small pig is born to Zuckerman's farm. It is so small that Fern's father prepares to kill it, while Fern saves it, names it Wilbur and keeps it as a pet. Wilbur finally grows too big to be a pet, so it is sent to Fern's uncle, Homer Zuckerman's farm. At Homer Zuckerman's farm Wilbur finds a lot of friends, among whom a spider named Charlotte is the best. Wilbur lives happily until one day he finds that he would be killed and made into bacon and ham in winter. Fortunately, Charlotte figures out a plan to save Wilbur.

The plans consists of three small plans. First, Charlotte weaves the words "some pig" in the middle of her spider web. This makes people think that Wilbur is something special. Second, Charlotte weaves another word "terrific" in the web, which makes Zuckerman believe Wilbur is such a terrific pig that he should take him to compete in the county fair. Third, Charlotte weaves into the web: "RADIANT". People flood to Homer Zuckerman's farm to see this radiant little pig. Finally, at the fair, Charlotte weaves in the web the word "humble". Everyone at the fair knows Wilbur is a humble pig. So Wilbur wins a special prize in the competition, and Homer will not kill such a pig for making bacon and ham.

Wilbur is saved but Charlotte is dying. Before Charlotte dies, she lays a sack of eggs. Wilbur saves Charlotte's babies by taking the sack of eggs back to the farm. Wilbur lives, and gets to see the coming of another spring and the birth of Charlotte's baby spiders.

☞ 3. Vocabulary

Direction: *Learn these new words and expression(s) from this movie and try to use them at EANLIC night.*

runt /rʌnt/   *n.* the smallest and least developed baby animal of a group born at the same time

(一胎中)最弱小的动物幼崽

barn /bɑːn/　*n*. a large farm building for storing crops, or for keeping animals in 谷仓,粮秣房,仓库;牲口棚

sniff /snɪf/　*v*. to breathe air in through your nose in order to smell something 嗅,闻

smokehouse /ˈsməʊkhaʊs/　*n*. a building or special construction for curing meat, fish, etc, by smoking (肉、鱼等的)烟熏室

slop /slɒp/　*n*. waste food that can be used to feed animals (喂动物的)食物残渣,泔水

cholera /ˈkɒlərə/　*n*. a serious disease that causes sickness and sometimes death. It is caused by eating infected food or drinking infected water 霍乱

frizzy /ˈfrɪzi/　*adj*. very tightly curled (头发)紧紧卷曲的

bloody /ˈblʌdi/　*adj.*, *adv*. used to emphasize what you are saying, in a slightly rude way 很,太,十分,非常(用于加强语气,略显粗鲁)

rodent /ˈrəʊdnt/　*n*. any small animal of the type that has long sharp front teeth, such as a rat or a rabbit 啮齿动物(如老鼠、兔子)

gnaw /nɔː/　*v*. to keep biting something hard 咬,啃

nocturnal /nɒkˈtɜːnl/　*adj*. (of animals) active at night (动物)夜行的,夜间活动的

converse /kənˈvɜːs/　*v*. to have a conversation with someone 谈话,交谈

drool /druːl/　*v*. to let saliva come out of your mouth 流口水,垂涎

anesthetize /æˈniːsθətaɪz/　*v*. to give someone an anesthetic so that they do not feel pain 使麻醉,给……施行麻醉

despise /dɪˈspaɪz/　*v*. to dislike and have a low opinion of someone or something 鄙视,看不起,蔑视

bouncy /ˈbaʊnsi/　*adj*. someone who is bouncy is always very happy, confident, and full of energy (人)生气勃勃的,精神饱满的,充满活力的

dud /dʌd/　*n*. something that is useless, especially because it does not work correctly 无用的东西,废物

yolk /jəʊk/　*n*. the yellow part in the center of an egg 蛋黄

ingrate /ˈɪŋɡreɪt/　*n*. an ungrateful person 忘恩负义者

slaughter /ˈslɔːtə(r)/　*v*. to kill an animal, especially for its meat 屠宰(动物)

scrumptious /ˈskrʌmpʃəs/　*adj*. food that is scrumptious tastes very good (食物)美味的,可口的

poultry /ˈpəʊltri/　*n*. birds such as chickens and ducks that are kept on farms in order to produce eggs and meat 家禽

abort /əˈbɔːt/　*v*. to stop an activity because it would be difficult or dangerous to continue it (因困难或危险)使(活动)中止

stealthy /ˈstelθi/　*adj*. moving or doing something quietly and secretly 悄悄的,鬼鬼祟祟的,偷偷的

radiant /ˈreɪdiənt/　*adj*. full of happiness and love, in a way that shows in your face and makes you look attractive 容光焕发的，喜悦的

flamingo /fləˈmɪŋɡəʊ/　*n.* a large pink tropical bird with very long thin legs and a long neck 红鹳，火烈鸟

peck /pek/　*v.* to move the beak forward quickly and hit or bite sth. （鸟）啄，啄食

humble /ˈhʌmbl/　*adj.* not considering yourself or your ideas to be as important as other people's 谦虚的，谦卑的

miraculous /mɪˈrækjələs/　*adj.* like a miracle, completely unexpected and very lucky 奇迹般的，不可思议的，不平凡的

languish /ˈlæŋɡwɪʃ/　*v.* to be forced to stay somewhere or suffer sth. unpleasant for a long time 变得衰弱；未能取得进展

pledge /pledʒ/　*n.* a serious promise or agreement, especially one made publicly or officially （尤指公开或正式做出的）誓言，誓约；保证

Expression(s)

rotten egg　臭鸡蛋，臭鸡蛋味
perk up　使振作；振作

☞ 4. Character description

Direction：Describe the main characters by using at least 5 adjectives in this movie with the reference of the words you have learned, and find examples in the movie to support your ideas (Table 6.1).

Table 6.1　Main Characters in *Charlotte's Web*

Main Characters	Adjectives	Examples
Wilbur		
Charlotte		
Fern		
The barn animals		
Templeton		

Section II In-class Tasks

☞ 1. Workshop

Direction：Discuss the questions with your classmates, and use the following sentence structures if it is possible.

Sentence structures for expressing doubt

- I'm not sure if ...
- I'm not convinced that ...
- I wonder if you realize that ...
- It's possible that ...
- It might be the case that ...
- Some people might argue that ...

(1) Why does Fern's father want to kill the piglet?

(2) How does Fern stop his father from killing the piglet?

(3) Who is Charlotte? Is Charlotte popular among the animals in the barn?

(4) What impression does the spider leave on the animals in the barn?

(5) Why do the animals in the barn call Wilbur a spring pig? What will be the fate of a spring pig?

(6) Why does Charlotte spin words on her web?

(7) What happens after people see "SOME PIG" on the web?

(8) Who's your favourite character in the movie?

2. Cloze

Direction：*Fill in the gaps in the following passages taken from the movie with the words or phrases given below.*

Passage 1

regular	passed	farm	plain	spring
order	change	special	astonishing	ordinary

There was nothing ___1___ about Somerset County. It was a deeply ___2___ place. No ___3___ thing ever happened there. The people who lived there were just ___4___ people. And the animals ... Well, they were just ___5___ old animals. They didn't question the ___6___ of things. So, the days ___7___, one very much like the other. But, one ___8___, on a small ___9___, a little girl did something, something that would ___10___ everything.

Passage 2

unusual	animals	kinder	changed	carried	sky	buds
promises	thaw	occasion	stillness	started	long	hardest
snowfall	circle	warmth	special	gestures	understanding	cold

Something had ___1___ in Somerset County. It was as if people knew they lived in a ___2___ place now. And, in small ways, they ___3___ being special people, a little bit

___4___, a bit more ___5___. And the ___6___ felt different, too closer. The ___7___ of their friendship ___8___ them through the ___9___, ___10___ months. They showed it in little ___11___ of kindness, ___12___ patience, and ___13___ kept. Even the ___14___ of hearts found themselves rising to the ___15___. And, finally, the greatest promise of all a spring pig saw his first ___16___. It was as though Charlotte herself had shaken it out of the ___17___. The ___18___ of winter continued to the first ___19___, like it always does. And then, the first ___20___ of spring. And, before you knew it, life had come full ___21___.

☞ 3. Story retelling

Direction: *Study the information in Reference 1 on SCQA of this unit, and then retell the story of* Charlotte's Web *by using specific details to support your ideas (Table 6.2).*

Table 6.2 SCQA in *Charlotte's Web*

SCQA Structure	Charlotte's Web
Situation: (How things are right now?)	
Complication: (A change in the situation)	
Question: (What gets raised by the complication?)	
Answer: (Resolution to the question)	

☞ 4. Sentence rearrangement

Direction: *Put the following sentences into the chronological order based on the story of* Charlotte's Web *(Table 6.3).*

Table 6.3 Sentences from *Charlotte's Web*

Orders	Sentences
	I can't have you keeping what will soon be a 300-pound pet around the house.
	Actually, in the world, if spiders didn't catch them, insects would take over the planet!
	A spring pig saw his first snowfall.
	You got to be quiet, okay? You're gonna get me in trouble.
	You made a spider beautiful to everyone in that barn.

continued

Orders	Sentences
	Fern was up before dawn, ridding the world of injustice.
	—I can crochet a doily. —Because someone taught you how. Nobody teaches a spider. They just know how to spin a web. The web itself is a miracle.
	I don't get that kind of royal treatment.
	I will treasure her memory forever.
	After a few weeks, the phenomenon of the web wore off. Nobody cared any more, and what was amazing yesterday was suddenly ordinary again today.
	Charlotte needed to think of something special. Special enough to change the way people saw the world, or at least one pig in the world, anyway.
	As we have all seen, humans have very short attention spans.

Section III English Chat Task

Direction: *Discuss the themes of this movie and organize your words on the specific themes* (Table 6.4).

Table 6.4 Themes of *Charlotte's Web*

Themes	Questions about Themes	Answers (Key Words for Each Question)
Admiration	• Does Wilbur deserve all the admiration he's getting? Why do you think he's an admirable pig? Or why might he not be quite so admirable? • Why do you think Charlotte gets ignored so much? Who admires her? Why doesn't she weave "SOME SPIDER" into her web? • What are the good things about being admired? How about the bad?	

continued

Themes	Questions about Themes	Answers (Key Words for Each Question)
Friendship	• How is Fern a good friend to Wilbur? And how is she a poor friend? What does this say about human-animal friendships? • Does Wilbur rely on his friends too much? Or does Charlotte rely on her friends too little? What does the movie suggest is the right balance between dependence and independence? • Is Wilbur always a good friend? Are there ways in which he is not a good friend?	
Perseverance	• Which human characters really value hard work? Are there certain characters that don't try very hard? • Why does Charlotte work so hard to save Wilbur? Are there any negative effects from all her hard work? What about the positive effects? • What is Templeton's attitude towards hard work?	
Mortality	• What is Charlotte's attitude towards death? How would you compare this to Wilbur's outlook on death? • Should the characters fight to stay alive or accept the fact that they'll eventually die? • Do the humans have a different outlook on death than the animals? How so?	
Time	• What do you think of the way changing seasons are represented? Do the changes sound good or bad? • In the movie, is there anything that stays the same over time? • How do the adult characters change over time?	

Section IV EANLIC Party Tasks

☞ **1. Give a presentation on the theme of *Charlotte's Web***

☞ **2. Role-play**

Direction: *Prepare this part in groups before class, and then do the role-play in class. Scan the QR code for role-play scripts.*

(1) The sow gives birth to 11 piglets. Fern's father decides to kill the runty one, but Fern stops her father and keeps the runty piglet.

(2) Charlotte's web helps Wilbur win a medal. She lays the egg sac and is dying …

(3) Wilbur begs Templeton to help him get Charlotte's egg sac.

☞ **3. Debate**

Direction: *Study the debate information in Reference 2 of this unit, and write a debate with a proper format.*

(1) Is it better to have a few close friends or a large group of acquaintances?

For: It is better to have a few close friends.

Against: It is better to have a large group of acquaintances.

(2) Should social media be considered a reliable platform for making and maintaining friendships?

For: Social media should be considered a reliable platform for making and maintaining friendships.

Against: Social media shouldn't be considered a reliable platform for making and maintaining friendships.

Section V After-class Tasks

☞ **1. Mindmap drawing**

Direction: *Read Reference 1 of this unit once again, and then draw a mindmap on the story of Charlotte's Web.*

☞ **2. Movie review**

Direction: *Design a "story sequence chart" of Charlotte's Web with the information of Reference 1. Scan the QR code for the addresses attached for your further study.*

References

☞ 1. SCQA: What is it? How does it work and how can it help you?

SCQA is a framework for structuring information. Using this framework, you can structure your message in a clear, attractive and narrative way. An SCQA has four basic elements. This makes it easy to learn and to use. **S, C, Q and A: the basic ingredients for a good story.** The four basic elements of an SCQA are Situation, Complication, Question and Answer. By connecting these elements, you create a logical story flow. By structuring your message as an SCQA, you present this idea as a solution to a problem. And you relate that problem to a situation with which your audience can identify. This makes your message clear, urgent and interesting. Using the SCQA structure, you'll communicate better and more easily.

The SCQA structure

- **Basic elements of the SCQA structure**
  - Situation: Function as a starting point and a common basis. Therefore, it primarily contains recognizable and agreed points.
  - Complication: Spell the reason for acting now. It contains threats/opportunities and the hurdles that need to be overcome.
  - Question: Ask the question how the hurdles of the C can be overcome. How to prevent the threat or seize the opportunity?
  - Answer: Provide the answer on how to overcome the hurdles. Explains how this will help deflect the threats or seize the opportunities.
- **Reasons for using an SCQA**
  - It will improve the process of making a story. You are more in control of the structure, which helps you decide what to include and what not to include. And it allows you to analyze how the different elements of your message are related.
  - It generally leads to a better result. A message with an SCQA is comprehensible and interesting and has a pleasant narrative arc. Also, your audience feels the urgency, which makes it more inclined to use your information.

☞ 2. How to write a debate speech?

A debate speech is a structured argument about a particular topic. It is conducted according to the set of rules designed to give each team a fair chance. Therefore, following a proper structure in debate writing is essential for the debater and the audience.

How to write a debate speech?

Develop a debate speech outline

Help to organize your main ideas. A speech outline consists of three main sections: introduction, body, and conclusion.

Write a speech introduction

Use an attention grabber. Involve a fact, quote, question, or story as an interesting first sentence to grab the audience's attention.

Open the debate. Open your debate by introducing the topic and making a clear statement to identify your position.

Present the context. Explain your position on the topic and which side you are supporting clearly. Furthermore, you can also discuss any real-life experiences that can relate to the topic.

Provide an overview of your arguments. State your arguments to help the audience understand the direction of your speech briefly.

Develop your key points in body paragraphs

Focus on the causes of the problem, the effects of the problem, expert opinion, examples, statistics, and present a solution.

Appeal to the motives and emotions of the listeners with a light touch. Ground examples in how people are affected.

Try to use rhetorical questions, which make your opponents consider the validity of their point.

Write a strong conclusion

Conclude a debate speech by referring back to the introduction and tying the conclusion into the same theme.

End a debate speech with quotations.

End a debate speech with a brief summation of the key arguments to ensure they remain fresh in judges' minds.

Unit 7

Coco

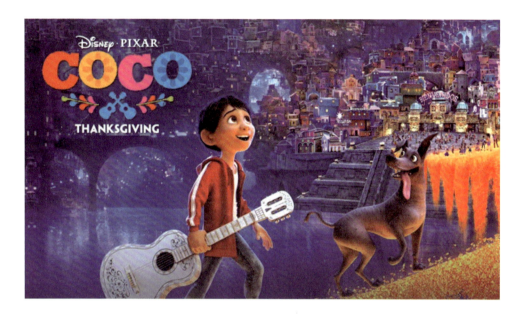

Unit Objectives:

1. Speaking skills:
   - Learn and be able to retell the story in this movie according to the Fichtean Curve structure.
   - Handle the method to present your debate with the given format.
2. Emotional objectives:
   - Cultivate students' love for family culture.
   - Foster a sense of pride for traditional culture.
   - Motivate students' awareness to protect good traditions.

Section I Pre-class Tasks

The students are supposed to watch the movie of *Coco* for at least 2 or 3 times ahead of the class, the first time for general understanding of the movie, and the second and third times for more detailed understanding and learning of English language, and then complete the following tasks before the class time.

☞ 1. Classic movie lines

Direction: *Read and recite the following lines from the movie.*

(1) Life is hard, but I have my guitar.
(2) No one was going to hand me my future. It was up to me to reach for my dream, grab it tight and make it come true.
(3) Success doesn't come for free. You have to do whatever it takes to seize your moment.

☞ 2. Background knowledge

Direction: *Go through the passage and prepare to share the information in class.*

Miguel is a 12-year-old boy, living in Santa Cecilia, Mexico. His great-great-grandmother, Imelda banished music from her life and started the family shoe-making business to provide for her daughter Coco (Miguel's great-grandmother), after his husband walked away with his guitar to pursue his dream: to play for the world. Given that music is banned in Miguel's family, he has a secret dream of becoming a musician like Ernesto de la Cruz, a popular actor and singer.

One day, Miguel removes Coco's photo with her parents. In the photo, he finds that Coco's father (whose face is torn out) was holding Ernesto's famous guitar. So he mistakes Ernesto as his great-great-grandfather. On the day of the dead, Miguel signs up for a talent show. He steals Ernesto's guitar and being cursed for stealing from the dead, he becomes invisible to everyone except his dog and his dead relatives who are visiting from the Land of the Dead for the holiday. Miguel's dead relatives find that because Miguel removes Imelda's photo from the ofrenda she cannot visit the land of the living, that Miguel is cursed for stealing Ernesto's guitar, and that he must receive a blessing from a member of his family using an Aztec marigold petal that can undo the curse or he will remain in the land of the dead. Imelda offers Miguel a blessing but on the condition that he abandons his musical pursuits. Miguel refuses and attempts to seek Ernesto's blessing.

Miguel meets Héctor, who once played with Ernesto and now is about to be forgotten by the living and disappear. Héctor offers to help Miguel find Ernesto on one condition that Miguel takes his photo back to the land of the living. Finally Miguel finds

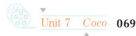

that Héctor is his great-great-grandfather and that it is Ernesto who poisoned Héctor and stole his song. Héctor and Imelda reconcile. With the help of Héctor, Imelda and other dead relatives, Miguel returns to the land of the living. He helps Coco bring back the memory of her father Héctor by playing a song that Héctor wrote for her during her childhood. Coco gives Miguel the torn-out piece of the photo from the ofrenda. Miguel's grandmother reconciles with him and accepts both Miguel and music back into the family.

☞ 3. Vocabulary

Direction: *Learn these new words from this movie and try to use them at EANLIC night.*

cursed /kɜːst/   *adj.* having a curse on it; suffering from a curse 被诅咒的

banish /ˈbænɪʃ/   *v.* to order sb. to leave a place, especially a country, as a punishment 放逐, 驱逐

apart /əˈpɑːt/   *adv.* separated by a distance, of space or time (指空间或时间)相隔,相距

dimple /ˈdɪmpl/   *n.* to make a hollow place appear on each of your cheeks, especially by smiling 酒窝,浅凹

bump /bʌmp/   *v.* to hit sb./sth. by accident 撞上,碰上

beloved /bɪˈlʌvd/   *adj.* loved very much by sb.; very popular with sb. 钟爱的;深受喜爱的

crush /krʌʃ/   *v.* to press or squeeze sth. so hard that it is damaged or injured, or loses tis shape 压坏,粉碎,挤压变形

giant /ˈdʒaɪənt/   *n.* a very large strong person who is often cruel and stupid 巨人

freak /friːk/   *n.* a person with a very strong interest in a particular subject 怪人

petal /ˈpetl/   *n.* part of the flower that is usually bright colored 花瓣

credit /ˈkredɪt/   *n.* praise, approval or honor 赞扬;赞许;荣誉

skeleton /ˈskelɪtn/   *n.* the frame of bones supporting a human or animal body 骨骼,骨架

sparkle /ˈspɑːkl/   *n.* to shine brightly with small flashes of light 闪烁,闪耀

falsify /ˈfɔːlsɪfaɪ/   *v.* to change something, such as a document, in order to deceive people 篡改,伪造(文件)

cactus /ˈkæktəs/   *n.* a plant that grows in hot dry regions especially one with thick stems covered in spines but without leaves 仙人掌

underestimate /ˌʌndərˈestɪmeɪt/   *v.* to fail to guess or understand the real cost, size, difficulty, etc. of something 低估,对……估计不足

sneak /sniːk/   *v.* to go somewhere secretly, or to take up someone or something somewhere secretly 偷偷地走,潜行

Plaza /ˈplɑːzə/   *n.* an open area or square in a town, especially in Spanish-speaking countries (尤指西班牙语国家城镇中的)露天广场

weird /wɪəd/   *adj.* very strange and unusual, unexpected or not natural 出乎意料的;超自然的,怪异的;不寻常的

brier /ˈbraɪə(r)/   *n.* a thorny stem or twig 荆棘

march /mɑːtʃ/ *v.* to walk with stiff regular steps like a soldier 齐步走，前进，行军

reunion /ˌriːˈjuːniən/ *n.* a situation when people meet again after they have not seen each other for a long time 团聚，重逢

gracias /ˈɡrɑːθiːɑːs/ *v.* (Spanish) to express thanks 谢谢

Chorizo /tʃəˈriːzəʊ/ *n.* (Spanish) sausage 香肠

esperate *v.* (Spanish) to wait 等待，等候

☞ 4. Character description

Direction：*Describe the main characters by using at least 5 adjectives in this movie with the reference of the words you have learned, and find examples in the movie to support your ideas (Table 7.1).*

Table 7.1　Main Characters in *Coco*

Main Characters	Adjectives	Examples
Miguel		
Héctor		
Coco		
Imelda		
Julio		

Section II In-class Tasks

☞ 1. Workshop

Direction：*Discuss the questions with your classmates, and use the following sentence structures if it is possible.*

Sentence structures for expressing disagreement

- I don't mean to be rude, but …
- No offense, but …
- Well, it's all nice and well, but …
- We'll just have to agree to disagree!
- Well, I can definitely see where you're coming from, but …
- With all due respect, but …

(1) What wrong things does Miguel do at the beginning of the movie? Have you done something that your family did not want you to do?

(2) What good things does Miguel do throughout the movie?

(3) Parents and their teen and preteen children certainly sometimes have issues over goals. Neither the parents nor the children handle it very well. What's wrong? What can I (or we) do to help them set and work on life goals?

(4) What do you know about your family history? Are there things you would like to know more about?

(5) Does Coco help you understand any of your friends better?

(6) How do you honor your family members in your unit?

☞ 2. Cloze

Direction: *Fill in the gaps in the following passage and song taken from the movie with the words or phrases given below.*

■ **Passage**

roped in	walk-away	provide	cursed	cry over
sing and dance	play for the world	rolled up	has torn … apart	musician
returned	banishing	count	wrestlers	shoes

Sometimes, I think I'm ___1___ ' cause of something that happened before I was even born. See, a long time ago, there was this family. The Pap, he was a ___2___. He and his family would ___3___ and ___4___ their blessings. But he also had a dream—to ___5___. And one day … he left with his guitar … and never ___6___. And my Mam… She didn't have time to ___7___ that ___8___ musician. After ___9___ all music from her life … she found a way to ___10___ for her daughter. She ___11___ her sleeves … and she learned to make shoes. She could have made candy or fireworks or sparkly underwear for ___12___. But no. She chose ___13___. Then she taught her daughter to make shoes. And later, she taught her son-in-law. Then her grandkids got ___14___. As her family grew, so did the business. Music ___15___ her family _____. But shoes held them all together.

■ **Song**

| my arms | far away | apart | goodbye | cry |
| the only way | secret | travel | sad guitar | heart |

Remember me
Though I have to say ___1___.
Remember me
Don't let it make you ___2___.
For even if I'm ___3___, I hold you in my ___4___.
I sing a ___5___ song to you each night we are ___6___.

Remember me
Though I have to ___7___ far.
Remember me
Each time you hear a ___8___.
Know that I'm with you ___9___ that I can be.
Until you're in ___10___ again.

☞ 3. Story retelling

Direction: Study the information in Reference 1 on the Fichtean Curve structure of this unit, and then retell the story of *Coco* by using specific details to support your ideas (Table 7.2).

Table 7.2 The Fichtean Curve Structure of *Coco*

The Fichtean Curve Structure	Coco
Raising action:	
Crisis 1	
Crisis 2	
Crisis 3	
The climax	
Falling action	

☞ 4. Sentence rearrangement

Direction: Put the following sentences into the chronological order based on the story of *Coco* (Table 7.3).

Table 7.3 Sentences from *Coco*

Orders	Sentences
	Only a song has the power to change a heart. Never underestimate the power of music.
	Music tore her family apart. Shoes brought them together.
	I had to have faith in my dream. No one was going to hand it to me. It was up to me to reach for that dream. Grab it tight and make it come true.
	If there's no one left in the living world to remember you, you disappear from this world. But you can change that!

continued

Orders	Sentences
	We may have our differences, but nothing's more important than family.
	Miguel, I give you my blessing, to go home and never forget how much your family cares for you.
	A melody played on the strings of our souls and the rhythm that rattled us down to the bone. Our love for each other will live on forever in every beat of my proud corazón.
	She didn't have time to cry over that walk-away musician. After banishing all music from her life ... she found a way to provide for her daughter. She rolled up her sleeves ... and she learned to make shoes.
	My pap used to sing me that song. He loved you, Mam Coco. Your pap loved you so much. I kept his letters, poems he wrote me.
	You've got to get home before sunrise or you'll be stuck here forever.

Section III English Chat Task

Direction: *Discuss the themes of this movie and organize your words on the specific themes (Table 7.4).*

Table 7.4 Themes of *Coco*

Themes	Questions about Themes	Answers (Key Words for Each Question)
Courage	• How does the theme of courage revealed in this movie? • What's your understanding of courage? What are its features?	
Death	• What's your understanding of death? • What does this movie say about it? Do you agree with it? Why or why not?	
Dream (Life goals)	• What are your dreams or life goals? • Have you and your parents fought over your dreams? • What could you do/have you done to achieve your life goals?	

continued

Themes	Questions about Themes	Answers (Key Words for Each Question)
Family values	• Do you know any of your family values? What are they? • What role does it play in your family? What are the good traditions in your family values? How could you apply them into your own life?	

Section IV EANLIC Party Tasks

☞ **1. Give a presentation on the theme of *Coco***

☞ **2. Role-play**

Direction: *Prepare this part in groups before class, and then do the role-play in class. Scan the QR code for role-play scripts.*

(1) When Miguel knows why his great-great-grandfather is not able to cross the bridge.

(2) Miguel sings the song for Mama Coco to help her remember her deceased father before her memory disappears.

☞ **3. Debate**

Direction: *Study the debate information in Reference 2 of this unit, and then present your debate with the given format.*

(1) Is death a natural and inevitable part of life, or can it be prevented or delayed indefinitely?

   For: Death is a natural and inevitable part of life.

   Against: Death can be prevented or delayed indefinitely.

(2) Is courage an innate trait or can it be developed and cultivated?

   For: Courage is an innate trait.

   Against: Courage can be developed and cultivated.

Section V After-class Tasks

☞ **1. Mindmap drawing**

Direction: *Read Reference 1 of this unit once again, and then draw a mindmap on the story* of Coco.

☞ 2. Movie review

Direction: *Design a "story map" about Coco with the help of Reference 1. Scan the QR code for the addresses attached for your further study.*

References

☞ 1. The Fichtean Curve structure

Do any search on story structure, and you will inevitably come up with the Fichtean Curve, one of the most basic and fundamental forms of plotting. It is a simple narrative structure used to describe a good story. It is a classic story structure that makes up almost every story. It contains three basic parts: rising action, the climax, and falling action.

The Fichtean Curve structure

Rising action

It refers to the part of your story that moves your characters closer to the climax. It is the primary part of the story and punctuated by several crises. After an "inciting incident", you must come up with new events from time to time to keep the narrative moving forward while maintaining a sense of tension. The inciting incident is the event that moves your central characters out of their comfort zones and into their journey through your story.

Crisis 1
Crisis 2
Crisis 3

With each new crisis, the hero faces bigger and better obstacles, each one of which should raise the stakes, become more personal to the protagonist, and progress the story towards the climax.

The climax

It should be the moment of most extreme tension in your story. At this point, the main character and the rest of the cast have no choice but to confront the main problem at hand. The stakes should be high, with characters facing a literal or figurative death.

Falling action

The characters have faced their final challenge and either triumphed or lost. It shows how different characters have been transformed by the climax. It shows the characters returning to a state of normalcy.

☞ 2. How to present a debate speech?

Whether you are a student, a policy-maker, or a business leader, the ability to debate effectively can be a game-changer. Here are the major components you need to present an effective debate speech.

- **How to present a debate speech?**
  - **Present with catchy introduction**
    - Starting you debate with a compelling introduction is important. You can begin with a question, a quote, or a statistic related to the topic.
    - State your stance on the topic and provide a preview of your arguments in your introduction.
  - **State the problem & Define key terms**
    - Define key terms in your speech that are important to your argument. This helps to ensure that your audience understands the meaning of the words you use.
  - **Present your arguments**
    - Start with your strongest argument and provide evidence to support it. Then, move on to the weaker arguments and provide evidence for each one.
    - A good argument often follows the PEE structure.
      - Point: State your main idea or argument, providing a concise and clear statement of your position. The point should be specific, focused, and relevant to the topic at hand.
      - Evidence: Provide supporting evidence to bolster your argument. You can use examples, statistics, or any other relevant information that helps illustrate your point.
      - Explanation: Elaborate on how the evidence you provided supports your point. This is where you explain the relationship between your point and the evidence, highlighting its significance.
  - **Address counterarguments through rebuttals**
    - Address counterarguments by acknowledging the opposing viewpoints and refuting them with evidence. It is a vital aspect of constructing a well-rounded and persuasive argument.
  - **Conclusion**
    - End your speech with a strong conclusion that summarizes your arguments and restates your stance on the topic. You can also end with a call to action, encouraging your audience to take action based on your argument.

Unit 8

Colorful Yunnan Tourism Paradise

Unit Objectives:

1. Speaking skills:
   - Develop the ability to deliver presentations on the unit topic.
   - Master the technique of conducting a debate, including tips on presenting a debate effectively.

2. Emotional objectives:
   - Instill love for the hometown.
   - Foster a sense of responsibility to introduce the hometown.

Section I Pre-class Tasks

The students are supposed to watch the video of *Colorful Yunnan Tourism Paradise* for at least 2 or 3 times ahead of the class, the first time for general understanding of the movie, and the second and third times for more detailed understanding and learning of English language, and then complete the following tasks before the class time.

☞ 1. Classic movie lines

Direction: *Read and recite the following lines from the movie.*

(1) Walk into Yunnan and let's unveil her mystery.

(2) Yunnan became one of the passages that China communicated outwards.

(3) Yunnan's charm will let you experience something new and out of the ordinary.

☞ 2. Background knowledge

Direction: *Go through the passage and prepare to share the information in class.*

Yunnan literally means "the place south of the colorful clouds". It is a province situated in the southwest of China. It borders countries such as Vietnam, Laos and Burma and provinces of China like Guizhou, Sichuan. It is a land with beautiful landscapes, natural resources and diversified culture.

The topography varies greatly with the altitude. Dividing Yunnan into two parts, east and west, we can see each has its unique features.

The east is the plateau area, which is the main component of the Yunnan-Guizhou Plateau. The average altitude is around 2,000 meters. It mainly features undulating low mountains and round hills. Basins are scattered among mountains, which are called "Bazi" by the locals. The basin areas are relatively flat with thick soil deposits and flowing rivers, so they are fertile and help develop the farming economy. Kunming, the capital city of Yunnan, is situated in one of these basins. In the west, the high mountains alternate with valleys, forming a precipitous landscape. The renowned Three Parallel Rivers lies in the northwest of Yunnan.

Yunnan is acclaimed as the "Plant Kingdom" and "Animal Kingdom". Because the diverse topographies nurture the greatest number of plant species (more than 18,000) as well as an incredible array of animals, including the Asian elephant and the protected golden monkey. It is also famous for its beautiful and spectacular natural scenery, such as the Jade Dragon Snow Mountain, the Tiger Leaping Gorge, the Meili Snow Mountain, and the Stone Forest.

Yunnan has the most ethnic minorities in China, which make up about 1/3 of the province's population. Of China's 55 ethnic minorities, the province is home to 51 and 25 of them exceed populations of 5,000. These ethnic minorities live together over vast areas while some live in concentrated communities. The residences of the ethnic minorities are various and characteristic, their clothes colorful and distinctive. Some of the ethnic groups have their own languages and writings. They celebrate varied and colorful festivals. The most famous ones include the Torch Festival of Yi Nationality, the March Fair of Bai Nationality, the Water-splashing Festival of Dai Nationality, the Zongge Festival of Jingpo Nationality and the Knife Pole Festival of Lisu Nationality, etc.

☞ 3. Vocabulary

Direction: *Learn these new words from this movie and try to use them at EANLIC night.*

remote /rɪˈməʊt/   *adj.* far away in distance or time 遥远的
mysterious /mɪˈstɪəriəs/   *adj.* strange and difficult to explain or understand 神秘的, 难理解的
paradise /ˈpærədaɪs/   *n.* heaven 天堂
altitude /ˈæltɪtjuːd/   *n.* the height of something above sea level 海拔
landform /ˈlændfɔːm/   *n.* a natural feature of a land surface 地貌
dwell /dwel/   *v.* to live in a particular place 居住
diversity /daɪˈvɜːsəti/   *n.* the condition of having or being composed of differing elements 多样性
harmony /ˈhɑːməni/   *n.* a situation in which people are friendly and peaceful, and agree with each other 和谐, 和睦
unveil /ˌʌnˈveɪl/   *v.* to remove the cover from something 揭开, 显露
Tibetan /tɪˈbetn/   *adj.* belonging or relating to Tibet, or to its people, language, or culture 藏族的
breed /briːd/   *v.* to bring up; to nurture 养育; 培育
heritage /ˈherɪtɪdʒ/   *n.* the traditional beliefs, values, customs, etc. of a family, group of people, or country 遗产, 传统
species /ˈspiːʃiːz/   *n.* a group of animals or plants of the same kind that can breed with each other 物种
gorge /gɔːdʒ/   *n.* a deep narrow valley with steep sides 峡谷
angle /ˈæŋgl/   *n.* the space between two lines or surfaces that join, measured in degrees 角, 角度
gigantic /dʒaɪˈgæntɪk/   *adj.* extremely large 巨大的, 庞大的
scale /skeɪl/   *n.* size or extent, especially when something is very big 规模, 范围
volcano /vɒlˈkeɪnəʊ/   *n.* a mountain from which hot melted rock, gas, steam, and ash from inside the earth sometimes burst 火山
plateau /ˈplætəʊ/   *n.* an area of flat land that is higher than the land around it 高原
matriarchy /ˈmeɪtrɪɑːki/   *n.* a social system that gives power and authority to women rather than men 母系制, 母系社会
dynasty /ˈdɪnəsti/   *n.* a period of years during which members of a particular family rule a

country 朝代

autonomous /ɔːˈtɒnəməs/ *adj.* able to govern itself or control its own affairs 自治的，有自治权的

fossil /ˈfɒsl/ *n.* the remains of an animal or a plant which have become hard and turned into rock 化石

sculpture /ˈskʌlptʃə(r)/ *n.* a work of art that is a solid figure or object made by carving or shaping wood，stone，clay，metal，etc. 雕像，雕塑品

Confucian /kənˈfjuːʃən/ *adj.* of or relating to the Chinese philosopher Confucius or his teachings or followers 儒家的；孔子学说的

pastoral /ˈpɑːstərəl/ *adj.* showing country life or the countryside，especially in a romantic way 田园的，乡村生活的

converge /kənˈvɜːdʒ/ *v.* to move towards a place from different directions and meet 聚集，集中

drift /drɪft/ *v.* to move along smoothly and slowly in water or air 漂流，漂移

☞ 4. Tourist attraction description

Direction：Describe tourist attractions by using at least 5 adjectives in this documentary with the reference of the words you have learned，and find examples in the video to support your ideas (Table 8.1).

Table 8.1　Information of Tourist Attractions

Tourist Attractions	Location	Description
The Stone Forest		
The Red Earth		
Lugu Lake		
Puzhehei/Baimei Village		
Dali Ancient City		
Fuxian Lake		

Section II　In-class Tasks

☞ 1. Workshop

Direction：Discuss the questions with your classmates，and use the following sentence structures if it is possible.

Topic sentence structures

- *One reason why ...*

- *The most important thing to remember is that ...*
- *Another important factor to consider is ...*
- *The first thing to note is that ...*
- *It's important to remember that ...*
- *Besides the previous point ...*

(1) Can you tell us Yunnan's geographic location and its weather?
(2) Why is Yunnan called "the kingdom of animals and plants"?
(3) What contributes to the cultural diversity of Yunnan?
(4) Which tourist attraction in Yunnan do you like most? Why?
(5) What does Yunnan's natural beauty originate from?
(6) In general, what does a tourist may experience in Yunnan?

2. Cloze

Direction: *Fill in the gaps in the following passages taken from the movie with the words or phrases given below.*

Passage 1

remote	reach	1,500	climate	southwestern	paradise	unique
diversity	mysterious		altitude	conventions	capital	landforms
access	dwell	direct flights		the kingdom of animals and plants		
structure	People's Republic of China			rare		

Yunnan, lying in the __1__ part of the __2__, is known as a __3__, __4__ and wonderful place. Yunnan is not out of __5__ and there is in fact easy __6__ to this region from almost every part of Asia. There are __7__ to Kunming, the __8__ city of Yunnan Province, from ... Republic of Korea, Thailand, Malaysia, Singapore, Myanmar, Laos, Vietnam, Cambodia and Bangladesh. Yunnan with an average __9__ of __10__ meters, is rich in geological __11__ and __12__, many of which are __13__ in the world. This consequently has an influence on the varied __14__ in Yunnan. A __15__ of animals and plants, Yunnan is rightfully called __16__ because of its effective ecological protection. Twenty-six minorities also __17__ here, and most of them have __18__ languages, writings, __19__ and religions which contributes to the cultural __20__ of this province.

Passage 2

pastoral	interpreting	majesty	journey	sigh
mankind	border	space	festivals	evolution
passed	carnivals	remains	purity	exploration

Come to Yunnan, you may choose an ecological ____1____ from which you may feel nature's ____2____, beauty, magic and ____3____. Come to Yunnan, and you will be in for a trip of national customs and traditions, feeling colorful national customs and being involved in the national ____4____ and ____5____. Come to Yunnan, feel her unique history and culture and you will ____6____ with the feeling the might of the historical ____7____ formed through two applied forces, ____8____ time and fixed ____9____. Come to Yunnan, join the journey of scenic ____10____ and it will open a window of exploring and ____11____ the ____12____ of nature and ____13____. Come to Yunnan, go back to the idyllic and ____14____ countryside and her fine natural ecology and simple customs will make you forget to return. Come to Yunnan, travel along the ____15____ and international rivers and you may enjoy Yunnan's specific border conditions and customs as well as experience those foreign sights.

☞ **3. Story retelling**

Direction: *Study the information in Reference 1 on the presentation structure of this unit, and then organize & prepare your presentation on* Colorful Yunnan Tourism Paradise *by using specific details to support your ideas* (*Table 8.2*).

Table 8.2 The Presentation Structure of *Colorful Yunnan Tourism Paradise*

The Presentation Structure	Colorful Yunnan Tourism Paradise
Introduction (Beginning): Give a preview of what you are going to say and how to gain the attention of the listeners with a statement of purpose.	
Main content (Middle): Arrange the key points in the logical order and expand them with supporting material—discussion, argument, analysis and appeal.	
Conclusion (End): Tell the audience what you have just told them (by summarizing the key points, concluding with the main subject and argument again by using different words).	

☞ **4. Sentence rearrangement**

Direction: *Put the following sentences into the chronological order based on the documentary of* Colorful Yunnan Tourism Paradise (*Table 8.3*).

Table 8.3 Sentences from *Colorful Yunnan Tourism Paradise*

Orders	Sentences
	For her magical sights, mysterious national customs and remote history, Yunnan Province has become the most diversified natural and cultural area in the world.
	Yunnan is the museum of natural wonders.
	Dali ancient city was once the capital of the great Nanzhao kingdom and Dali kingdom.
	The ancient city of Lijiang, locating at the foot of the snow mountain, is a water city.
	Shangri-La re-named after the novel *The Lost Horizon* by James Hilton. Tibetan nationality living in the place quite near to the sky and in the purest ideal world.
	Jianshui old city and its huge and ancient architecture clusters are the living fossils of modern Yunnan culture.
	Dianchi Lake in Kunming is the biggest plateau lake in Yunnan.
	Yunnan abounds with mountains and hills, which amount to 94% of its 394,000 square kilometers. All of them are different and contribute Yunnan subtle natural beauty.
	The Three Parallel Rivers is a world natural heritage site.
	The Confucian Temple in Jianshui is the second biggest in China and it is in good condition.
	Colorful Yunnan, tourism paradise.

Section III English Chat Task

Direction: *Discuss the themes of this video and organize your words on the specific themes (Table 8.4).*

Table 8.4 Themes of *Colorful Yunnan Tourism Paradise*

Themes	Questions about Themes	Answers (Key Words for Each Question)
Geographical condition	• Where does Yunnan locate in China? • Can you describe what the weather is like in Yunnan?	

continued

Themes	Questions about Themes	Answers (Key Words for Each Question)
Fame of Yunnan	• What fame does Yunnan enjoy in China? • How come Yunnan enjoy such reputations?	
Access to Yunnan	• Is it convenient for a foreigner to go to Yunnan? Why? • What means of transport would you suggest to go to Yunnan? Why?	
Tourist attractions	• What tourist attractions are there in Yunnan? Can you name some of them? • Which tourist attraction would you like to recommend most to a foreign tourist? Can you describe it in detail?	
Culture	• How many ethnic groups are there in Yunnan? Can you tell us some unique culture and customs of a particular ethnic minority? • What religions do people mainly practise in Yunnan?	

Section IV EANLIC Party Tasks

☞ **1. Give a presentation on the theme of** *Colorful Yunnan Tourism Paradise*

☞ **2. Make a "promotional video" of your hometown**

Direction: *Make a "promotional video" of your hometown with captions with the information in Reference 3 in groups before class, and then share the videos at EANLIC night.*

☞ **3. Debate**

Direction: *Study the debate information in Reference 2 of this unit, and then conduct your debate with tips on presenting it effectively.*

（1）Should Yunnan prioritize sustainable tourism over industrialization?

For: Yunnan should prioritize sustainable tourism.

Against: Yunnan should prioritize industrialization.

（2）Is overtourism a consequence of tourism's success or a failure of tourism in management?

For: Overtourism is a consequence of tourism's success in management..

Against: Overtourism is a failure of tourism in management.

Section V After-class Tasks

☞ 1. Mindmap drawing

Direction: *Read Reference 1 of this unit, and then draw a mindmap on* Colorful Yunnan Tourism Paradise.

☞ 2. Promotional video making

Direction: *Design and make a promotional video about a local product with the information of Reference 3.*

References

☞ 1. What is a presentation?

We define a presentation as a means of communication that can be adapted to various speaking situations, such as talking to a group, addressing a meeting or briefing a team. Effective presentations usually require careful thought and preparation.

Presentation explains what information you need before you can really start to plan your presentation and decide what you are going to say. The most important aspects include the objective of the presentation, the subject, and the audience.

Irrespective of whether the occasion is formal or informal, you should always aim to give a clear, well-structured delivery. To do so, you need to organize your presentation material. You can either do this in your head, or use a technique like mind-mapping to help you identify links and good flow.

By the time you come to write your presentation, you should know exactly what you want to say and the order in which you want to say it. You may want to use one of the standard presentation structures, such as "what, why, how?" You will also find it helpful to consider how to tell your story most effectively, and to use stories in your presentation to illustrate points. There is more about this in our page on writing your presentation.

You also need to decide on your presentation method. Presentations range from the formal to the informal. Your choice of presentation method will depend on many factors, including the audience, the venue, the facilities, and your own preferences.

How to structure a presentation?

Basic starting points

- Give your presentation an introduction, a main message, and a conclusion.
- Think about using stories to get your message across.
  - Try to think about your presentation as telling a story to your audience. What is the point that you are trying to make, and how can you best get it across?
  - Use theme-related stories in your presentation to draw your audience in and to illustrate each point you want to make.

Structure your presentation

- Harness the power of three.
  - Structure your presentation by using the magic number of three, for the brain finds it relatively easy to grasp three points at a time.
  - Include the three main elements: the introduction, middle and conclusions in your presentation. Within the main body of your presentation, divide your key message into three elements and then expand each of these points into three sub-points.
- Use "what?", "why?" and "how?" questions.
  - "What?" identifies the key message you wish to communicate. The benefits of your message: What will they gain, what can they do with the information, and what will the benefit be?
  - "Why?" addresses the next obvious question that arises for the audience. Having been told "what", the audience will naturally start to think "Why should I do that?", "Why should I think that?" or "Why should that be the case?"
  - "How?" is the final question that naturally arises in the audience's mind. They want to know how they are going to achieve what you have just suggested. Instead of telling people how they should act on your message, offer suggestions or examples to follow.

Presentation can be divided into three sections.

Presentation

Introduction (Beginning)

- Give a preview of what you are going to say and how to gain the attention of the listeners with a statement of purpose.
- Tell the audience in the introduction what your subject is and how you have organized the presentation (by stating the key elements).

Main content (Middle)

- Arrange the key points in the logical order and expand them with supporting material—discussion, argument, analysis and appeal.
- Tell your audience the details of the key elements and/or messages (by expanding and qualifying the key points in more detail and providing supporting evidence).

Conclusion (End)

- Tell the audience what you have just told them (by summarizing the key points, concluding with the main subject and argument again by using different words).

☞ 2. Tips on presenting a debate speech effectively

We have learned how to present a debate speech in the last unit. In this unit we will learn how to improve it even better with the tips below.

☞ 3. Promotional video

Promotional videos are top forms of online mass communication desired by Internet users. Any organization with a website is aware that having online video is needed—consumers demand it. Fortunately, with inexpensive cameras, powerful mobile devices and the high speed

Internet, promotional videos are easier than ever to create, distribute and view. When we watch a promotional video, we should pay attention to the following aspects.

◆ The purpose: What is the primary goal? To communicate? To promote business? To attract tourists? To advertise a particular organization or place?

◆ Information: What is the main core message?

◆ Target viewers: Who is the primary target audience? Age? Interests? Income? Whether it is worth watching?

◆ Resources: Where can you find such a video when you need it? TV program? Online video?

Unit 9　*Wild China* (Episode 1, *Heart of the Dragon*)

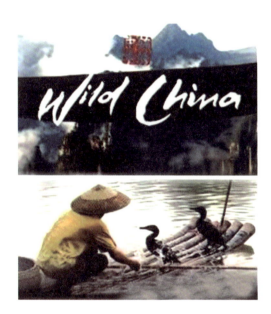

Unit Objectives:

1. Speaking skills:
   - Learn how to effectively organize and deliver a presentation on the documentary.
   - Master the technique of delivering a debate with strong opening statements.
2. Emotional objectives:
   - Cultivate love for China.
   - Instill a sense of responsibility for environmental protection at home and abroad.
   - Foster a sense of pride in Chinese culture.

Section I Pre-class Tasks

The students are supposed to watch the documentary of *Wild China* (Episode 1, *Heart of the Dragon*) for at least 2 or 3 times ahead of the class, the first time for general understanding of the movie, and the second and third times for more detailed understanding and learning of English language, and then complete the following tasks before the class time.

1. Classic movie lines

Direction: *Read and recite the following lines from the movie.*
(1) Chinese civilization is the world's oldest and today it's the largest.
(2) Given the right help, even the rarest creatures can return from the brink.
(3) If we show the will, nature will find the way.

2. Background knowledge

Direction: *Go through the passage and prepare to share the information in class.*

"We want the Chinese to feel proud of their countryside and wildlife, to care about it and to seek to ensure its survival. We also hope to redress the negative view of China's environment propagated in Western media."

—Series Producer Phil Chapman, writing in BBC *Wildlife* magazine

Wild China is a 6-episode documentary co-produced for the first time by the BBC Natural History Unit and China Central Television (CCTV). It films 56 national wildlife reserves and landscape conservation zones, 86 species of rare wild animals and plants and stories about the life of over 30 ethnic groups, showing the natural and cultural landscapes of China. It employs advanced filming technology such as aerial photography, infrared photography, high-speed photography, time lapse photography and underwater photography to record lots of precious and splendid scenes.

With wildlife filmmaking in its infancy in China, and a perception in the developed world of a country plagued by environmental problems, the producers hoped that the series would change attitudes in both the East and the West. Filming for the series took place over 16 months, and involved half a million miles of travel on 57 separate filming trips to some of China's most inaccessible and spectacular locations. The production team shot over 500 hours of HD footage in 26 of China's 30 provinces.

Despite being granted unprecedented access to many remote and protected areas, one of the main challenges faced by the filmmakers was finding wildlife. Although 15% of China's territory has some form of protection, this is not a guarantee of safety for wildlife, as reserves were often found to be under-equipped and under-staffed. In addition, they encountered a lack of local expertise and specialist knowledge, as few of China's zoologists were naturalists with an interest in observing wildlife. Producers even struggled to film the courting behavior of one of the country's commonest creatures, the rice-paddy frog. Consequently, the team's attempts to find and film wildlife were not always successful.

With the support of local party officials, the producers found it easier to contact and film local people. They were particularly keen to record examples of traditional lifestyles which incorporate the natural world to give the series a cultural context. The episodes were divided by region to present the distinct cultural as well as ecological differences.

☞ 3. Vocabulary

Direction: *Learn these new words from this movie and try to use them at EANLIC night.*

harbor /ˈhɑːbə/ *n.* an area of water on the coast, protected from the open sea by strong walls, where ships can shelter 港口, 港湾

     v. to contain sth. and allow it to develop 包含, 藏有

exotic /ɪɡˈzɒtɪk/ *adj.* from or in another country, especially a tropical one; seeming exciting and unusual because it is connected with foreign countries 来自异国的(尤指热带国家); 奇异的; 异国情调的

motif /məʊˈtiːf/ *n.* a design or a pattern used as a decoration 装饰图案, 装饰图形

cultivate /ˈkʌltɪveɪt/ *v.* to grow plants or crops 种植, 栽培, 培育

plunge /plʌndʒ/ *v.* (of prices, temperatures, etc.) to decrease suddenly and quickly 暴跌, 骤降, 突降

feat /fiːt/ *n.* an action or a piece of work that needs skill, strength or courage 技艺, 武艺, 功绩, 英勇事迹

approach /əˈprəʊtʃ/ *v.* to come near to sb./sth. in distance or time (在距离或时间上)靠近, 接近

predator /ˈpredətə(r)/ *n.* an animal that kills and eats other animals; a person or an organization that uses weaker people for their own advantage 掠夺者; 捕食性动物; 实行弱肉强食的人(或机构); 剥削者

slaughter /ˈslɔːtə(r)/ *n.* the killing of animals for their meat; the cruel killing of large numbers of people at one time, especially in a war 屠宰; 宰杀; (尤指战争中的)屠杀, 杀戮

dominate /ˈdɒmɪneɪt/ *v.* to control or have a lot of influence over sb./sth., especially in an unpleasant way 支配, 控制, 左右, 影响

fertile /ˈfɜːtaɪl/ *adj.* (of land or soil) that plants grow well in; (of people, animals or plants) that can produce babies, young animals, fruit or new plants 肥沃的, 富饶的; 能生育的; 可繁殖的; 能结果的

chitchat /ˈtʃɪttʃæt/ *n.* informal talk about things that are not very important 闲聊

oblivious /əˈblɪviəs/ *adj.* not aware of sth. 不知道的, 未注意的, 未察觉的

transplant /trænsˈplɑːnt/ *v.* to take an organ, skin, etc. from one person, animal, part of the body, etc. and put it into or onto another 移植(器官、皮肤等)

scarce /skeəs/ *adj.* not enough of it and it is only available in small quantities 缺乏的, 不足的, 稀少的

erosion /ɪˈrəʊʒn/ *n.* the gradual destruction and removal of rock or soil in a particular area by rivers, the sea, or the weather 侵蚀

dissolve /dɪˈzɒlv/ *v.* to make a solid become part of a liquid 使(固体)溶解

conceal /kənˈsiːl/ *v.* to hide sb./sth. 隐藏, 隐瞒, 掩盖

ultimate /ˈʌltɪmət/ *adj.* happening at the end of a long process 最后的, 最终的, 终极的

subsequently /ˈsʌbsɪkwəntli/ *adv.* afterwards; later; after something else has happened 随后; 后来; 之后, 接着

vertical /ˈvɜːtɪkl/ *adj.* going straight up or down from a level surface or from top to bottom in a picture, etc. 竖的, 垂直的, 直立的

groom /gruːm/ *v.* to clean or brush an animal; to clean the fur or skin of another animal or itself (给动物)擦洗, 刷洗; 理毛, 梳毛

irresistible /ˌɪrɪˈzɪstəbl/ *adj.* so strong that it cannot be stopped or resisted 不可遏止的, 无法抵制的

inaccessible /ˌɪnækˈsesəbl/ *adj.* difficult or impossible to reach or to get 难以达到的, 不可得到的

enterprising /ˈentəpraɪzɪŋ/ *adj.* having or showing the ability to think of new projects or new ways of doing things and make them successful 有事业心的, 有进取心的, 有创业精神的

boarder /ˈbɔːdə(r)/ *n.* a child who lives at school and goes home for the holidays 在学校寄宿的学生, 寄宿生

orientate /ˈɔːrienteɪt/ *v.* to face or turn to the east 朝向, 面向, 使朝东

edible /ˈedəbl/ *adj.* fit or suitable to be eaten; not poisonous 适宜食用的; (无毒而)可以吃的

resilient /rɪˈzɪliənt/ *adj.* able to feel better quickly after something unpleasant such as shock, injury, etc. 可迅速恢复的, 有适应能力的

delicacy /ˈdelɪkəsi/ *n.* a type of food considered to be very special in a particular place 精美的食物, 佳肴

extinct /ɪkˈstɪŋkt/ *adj.* (of a type of plant, animal, etc.) no longer in existence 不再存在的, 已灭绝的, 绝种的

amphibian /æmˈfɪbiən/ *n.* any animal that can live both on land and in water 两栖动物

epitomize /ɪˈpɪtəmaɪz/ *v.* to be a perfect example of sth. 成为……的典范(或典型)

descendant /dɪˈsendənt/ *n.* a person's descendants are their children, their children's children, and all the people who live after them who are related to them 后裔, 后代, 子孙

self-sufficient /ˌself səˈfɪʃnt/ *adj.* able to do or produce everything that you need without the help of other people 自给自足的, 自立的

☞ 4. Description

Direction: *Describe the main items by using at least 5 adjectives in this documentary with the reference of the words you have learned, and find examples in the video to support your ideas (Table 9.1).*

Table 9.1 Items in *Wild China* (Episode 1, *Heart of the Dragon*)

Items	Adjectives	Examples
China		
Li River		
Karst landscape		
Rice cultivation		

Section II In-class Tasks

☞ 1. Workshop

Direction: *Discuss the questions with your classmates, and use the following sentence structures if it is possible.*

Sentence structures for scientific study
- The cause of _____ was …
- The effect of _____ was …
- The data shows …
- The benefits of this _____ are …
- Based on _____, we can conclude that …
- From this research, we can conclude …
- The results proved that …

(1) What does the swallow mean to the Miao people?
(2) How big is the vast area of southwest China?
(3) What is the defining image of southern China?
(4) What is concealed beneath the visible landscape of the karst? What do they mean to Chinese explorers?
(5) Caves are usually shelters for animals. What are their other functions?
(6) How does a Rickett's mouse-eared bat catch fishes?
(7) Why is the Chinese giant salamander of Zhangjiajie called the baby fish?
(8) How does the weather differ between north and south China in November?

2. Cloze

Direction: *Fill in the gaps in the following passages taken from the movie with the words or phrases given below.*

Passage 1

exotic	travelers	magical	mind-numbing	harboring
hidden	partnership	environmental	explore	50
social	remarkable	creatures	highest mountains	searing

The last ___1___ world, China. For centuries, ___2___ to China have told tales of ___3___ landscapes and surprising ___4___. Chinese civilization is the world's oldest and today, its largest, with well over a billion people. It's home to more than ___5___ distinct ethnic groups and a wide range of traditional lifestyles, often in close ___6___ with nature. We know that China faces immense ___7___ and ___8___ problems. But there is great beauty here, too. China is home to the world's ___9___, vast deserts ranging from ___10___ hot to ___11___ cold. Steaming forests ___12___ rare creatures. Grassy plains beneath vast horizons, and rich tropical seas. Now for the first time ever, we can ___13___ the whole of this great country, meet some of the surprising and ___14___ creatures that live here and consider the relationship of the people and wildlife of China to the ___15___ landscape in which they live.

Passage 2

competition	species	round trip	symbolize	proof
welcoming	endangered	resources	refuge	chilly
exploitation	9,000	resilient	long-distance	space

By November, northern China is becoming distinctly ___1___. But the south is still relatively warm and ___2___. Across the vast expanse of Poyang Lake, the birds are gathering. Tundra swans are ___3___ migrants from northern Siberia. To the Chinese, they ___4___ the essence of natural beauty. The Poyang Lake Nature Reserve offers winter ___5___ to more than a quarter of a million birds from more than 100 ___6___, creating one of southern China's finest wildlife experiences. The last birds to arrive at Poyang are those which have made the longest journey to get here, all the way from the Arctic coast of Siberia. The Siberian crane, known in China as the white crane, is seen as a symbol of good luck. Each year, almost the entire world population of these critically ___7___ birds make a ___8___-kilometer ___9___ to spend the winter at Poyang. Like the white cranes, many of south China's unique animals face pressure from ___10___ and ___11___ with people over ___12___ and ___13___. But if China is living ___14___ of anything, it is that wildlife is surprisingly ___15___ . Given the right help, even the rarest creatures can return from the brink. If we show the will, nature will find the way.

☞ 3. Story retelling

Direction: *Study the information in Reference 1 on documentary of this unit, and then retell the information of* Wild China *by using specific details to support your ideas* (*Table 9.2*).

Table 9.2 Documentary Structure of *Wild China* (Episode 1, *Heart of the Dragon*)

Documentary Structure	*Wild China* (Episode 1, *Heart of the Dragon*)
Purpose: To teach us more about the world around us. To give us a unique perspective on the lives of people. To inspire compassion in its viewers.	
Introduction: To captivate the audience and make them want to watch more. It is a great opportunity to tell the audience what the documentary movie is about and what you will be including in the main section.	
Main Section: To explore the topic and to pick out the interesting information or the moments it would like to present to the audience. The aim is to present information that the audience may not know and to promote the movie.	
Conclusion: To summarize the main points and bring the story to a natural end, leaving the audience feeling informed. This may include the answer to a question asked in the introduction, or the end of a journey started in the introduction.	

☞ 4. Sentence rearrangement

Direction: *Put the following sentences into the chronological order based on the documentary of* Wild China *(Episode 1,* Heart of the Dragon*) (Table 9.3).*

Table 9.3   Sentences from *Wild China* (Episode 1, *Heart of the Dragon*)

Orders	Sentences
	The Chinese have been cultivating rice for at least 8 thousand years.
	For centuries, travelers to China have told tales of magical landscapes and surprising creatures.
	There is a saying in the far south. We will eat anything with legs, except a table and anything with wings, except a plane.
	This natural wonder has become a famous tourist spot, receiving close to 2 million visitors each year.
	In Chinese rural life everything has a use.
	Exploring a cave is like taking the journey through time.
	These monkeys are spectacularly good rock climbers from the time they learnt to walk.
	The Chinese are fond of curiously shaped rocks.
	A limestone terrain which has become the defining image of southern China.
	Much of this hidden world has never been seen by human eyes.
	Swallow pairs remain faithful for life.
	The answer to extinction is protection.

Section III   English Chat Task

Direction: *Discuss the themes of this video and organize your words on the specific themes (Table 9.4).*

Table 9.4 Themes of *Wild China* (Episode 1, *Heart of the Dragon*)

Themes	Questions about Themes	Answers (Key Words for Each Question)
China	• How do you understand the expression "the last hidden world, China"? • How to briefly introduce China?	
Environmental protection in China	• How do you understand the sentence "If we show the will, nature will find the way"? • What environmental problems does China face today? Do you think the measures taken by the Chinese government to protect the environment are effective? Why or why not?	
Li River of Guilin	• How does Li River of Guilin strike you? • What is the traditional way of catching fishes for the fishermen on the Li River?	
Endangered animals in China	• Can you give us at least two examples of endangered animals from the documentary? • What is their current condition?	
Purposes of filming *Wild China* (Episode 1, *Heart of the Dragon*)	• What do you think are the purposes of filming *Wild China* (Episode 1, *Heart of the Dragon*)? • After watching *Wild China* (Episode 1, *Heart of the Dragon*), how should we react?	

Section IV EANLIC Party Tasks

☞ **1. Give a presentation on the theme of *Wild China* (Episode 1, *Heart of the Dragon*)**

☞ **2. Role-play**

Direction: Learn the opening remarks of this documentary, and then explain it to your classmates in the role of narrator and audience. Scan the QR code for role-play scripts.

3. Debate

Direction: *Study the debate information in Reference 2 of this unit, and then deliver your debate with "strong opening statements".*

(1) Can humans stop global warming in next ten years?

For: Humans can stop global warming in the next ten years.

Against: Humans cannot stop global warming in the next ten years.

(2) Is it moral to keep wild animals in the zoo?

For: It is moral to keep wild animals in the zoo.

Against: It is not moral to keep wild animals in the zoo.

Section V After-class Tasks

1. Mindmap drawing

Direction: *Read Reference 1 of this unit once again, and then draw a mindmap of* Wild China (*Episode 1*, Heart of the Dragon).

2. Movie review

Direction: *Enjoy reading the movie review sample of this documentary. Scan the QR code for the movie review sample and addresses attached for your further study.*

References

1. Documentary

Documentaries are a powerful tool for preserving history and stories for future generations. A good documentary film preserves, teaches, and entertains. It can give us a unique perspective on the lives of people in the past. A good documentary film manages to inspire compassion in its viewers.

Documentaries are usually well researched, planned, and executed. They connect viewers to the story and the subject. Every documentary is a narrative film because it either tells a story or uses one to make a point.

Documentaries usually include interviews, narration, and sometimes short re-enacted scenes that explain what the interviewees are saying. Like any good story, a documentary needs a strong beginning, middle, and end.

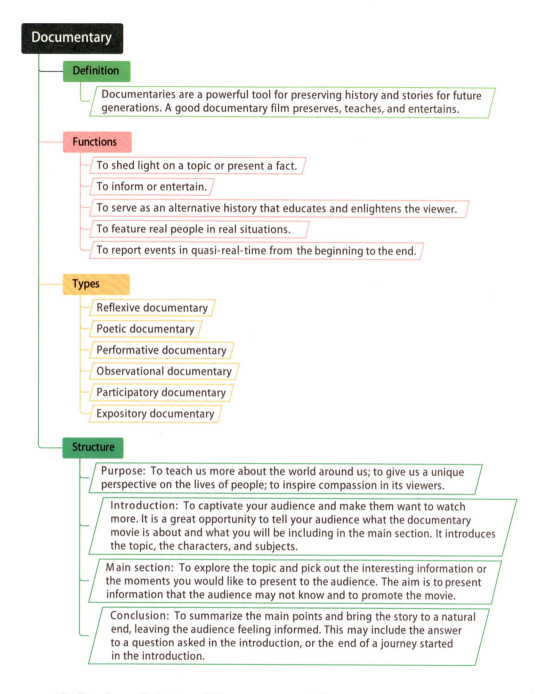

2. Begin a debate with strong opening statements

The opening statement introduces the subject matter of the discussion and sets the pace for the body of the debate, where the speaker extensively discusses his views. The opening statement serves as a background for the audience to have a better understanding of the discussion.

Every good speech and discussion starts with a strong sentence; hence start your debate with strong opening lines that can help you impress the audience and the judge immediately. An opening statement is to start your debate by giving your audience a roadmap into the rest of the discourse. Using the opening statement as a strategy to achieve this requires that you have a holistic overview of what you intend to say. With this technique, you present an opening that draws the audience to the direction you want. You also have to get them curious enough to follow you through to the end of the discussion. You can learn more about it in the following mindmap.

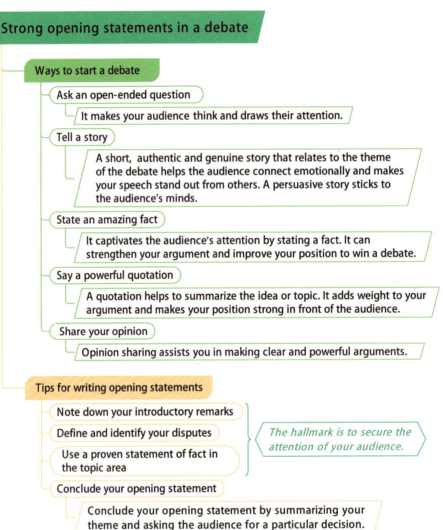

Unit 10

Blue Planet II (Episode 1)

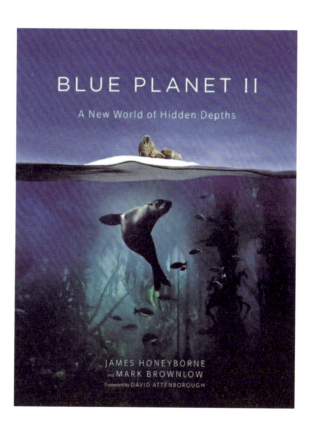

Unit Objectives:

1. Speaking skills:
   - Learn how to effectively tell documentary stories.
   - Develop the ability to rebut a debate more effectively.
2. Emotional objectives:
   - Cultivate love for marine creatures.
   - Instill love and appreciation for the natural world.
   - Foster awareness about the importance of protecting the local environment and promoting biological diversity.

Section I Pre-class Tasks

The students are supposed to watch the documentary of *Blue Planet II* (Episode 1) for at least 2 or 3 times ahead of the class, the first time for general understanding of the movie, and the second and third times for more detailed understanding and learning of English language, and then complete the following tasks before the class time.

☞ 1. Classic movie lines

Direction: *Read and recite the following lines from the movie.*

(1) Solving these problems together helps create a bond so strong that the mother will stay in contact with her young for the rest of her life.

(2) The oceans, seemingly limitless, invoke in us a sense of awe, and wonder, and also sometimes, fear.

(3) Creating an extraordinary ballet of life and death.

☞ 2. Background knowledge

Direction: *Go through the passage and prepare to share the information in class.*

Blue Planet II is a 2017 British natural documentary series on marine life produced by the BBC Natural History Unit. Like its predecessor, *The Blue Planet* (2001), it is narrated and presented by naturalist Sir David Attenborough.

The filming of the series spans more than four years, involving 125 expeditions across 39 countries and producing more than 6,000 hours of underwater dive footage from over an estimated 4,000 dives.

In China, the series is broadcast at Tencent's QQ Live from 30 October, 2017, with episodes updating every Monday at 18:00. It is also broadcast on China Central Television's documentary channel, CCTV-9, with episodes airing each Monday from 6 November, 2017 at 21:00.

"We are at a unique stage in our history. Never before have we had such an awareness of what we are doing to the planet, and never before have we had the power to do something about that. Surely we have a responsibility to care for our blue planet. The future of humanity, and indeed all life on Earth, now depends on us," said David Attenborough.

The program has been credited with raising awareness of plastic pollution both domestically and internationally, an influence dubbed the "Blue Planet effect". Following the program's airing in the UK, the BBC announced its intention to completely ban single-use plastics within its organization by 2020. In April 2018, in response to growing public support directly linked to *Blue Planet II*, the British government announces considering a national ban on single-use plastic products.

It is reported that the number of people in China simultaneously streaming *Blue Planet II* (approximately 80 million) has a noticeable impact upon the Internet speed within the country. The popularity of the documentary in China is cited as partly the reason British Prime Minister Theresa May gives Chinese president Xi Jinping a *Blue Planet II* box set signed by David Attenborough. It is also symbolic of a joint plan to tackle plastic pollution and the illegal wildlife trade, announced by British officials during Xi's 2018 visit.

3. Vocabulary

Direction: *Learn these new words from this movie and try to use them at EANLIC night.*

surface /ˈsɜːfɪs/ *n.* the outside or top layer of something 表面，表层

creature /ˈkriːtʃə(r)/ *n.* a living thing, real or imaginary, which can move around, such as an animal 生物

revolutionary /ˌrevəˈluːʃənəri/ *adj.* connected with political revolution; involving a great or complete change 革命的；彻底变革的，巨变的

crucial /ˈkruːʃl/ *adj.* extremely important, because it will affect other things 至关重要的，关键的

reveal /rɪˈviːl/ *v.* to make sth. known to sb. 揭示，显示

episode /ˈepɪsəʊd/ *n.* one part of a story that is broadcast on television or radio in several parts（电视连续剧或无线电广播剧的）一集

tropics /ˈtrɒpɪks/ *n.* the region between the tropics of Cancer and Capricorn 热带（北、南回归线之间的地带）

conceal /kənˈsiːl/ *v.* to hide sb./sth. 隐藏，隐瞒，掩盖

coral /ˈkɒrəl/ *n.* a hard substance that is red, pink or white in colour, and that forms on the bottom of the sea from the bones of very small creatures 珊瑚

deliberately /dɪˈlɪbərətli/ *adv.* done in a way that was planned, not by chance 故意，蓄意

reluctant /rɪˈlʌktənt/ *adj.* hesitating before doing sth. because you do not want to do it or because you are not sure that it is the right thing to do 不情愿的，勉强的

antimicrobial /ˌæntɪmaɪˈkrəʊbɪəl/ *adj.* destroying or inhibiting the grow of microorganisms and especially pathogenic microorganisms 抗微生物的

infection /ɪnˈfekʃn/ *n.* the act or process of causing or getting a disease 传染，感染

intimate /ˈɪntɪmət/ *adj.* having a close and friendly relationship 亲密的，密切的

shallow /ˈʃæləʊ/ *adj.* not having much distance between the top or surface and the bottom; not showing serious thought, feelings, etc. about sth. 浅的；肤浅的，浅薄的

density /ˈdensəti/ *n.* the quality of being dense; the degree to which sth. is dense; (physics) the thickness of a solid, liquid or gas measured by its mass per unit of volume 密集；浓度；密度

inevitable /ɪnˈevɪtəbl/ *adj.* something that you cannot avoid or prevent 不可避免的，不能防止的

juvenile /ˈdʒuːvənaɪl/　　n. a young person who is not yet an adult 少年

　　　　　　　　　　　adj. connected with young people who are not yet adults 少年的,未成年的

solitary /ˈsɒlətri/　adj. done alone; without other people 独自的;单独的

evaporate /ɪˈvæpəreɪt/　v. if a liquid evaporates or if something evaporates it, it changes into a gas, especially steam (使)蒸发,挥发

generate /ˈdʒenəreɪt/　v. to produce or create sth. 产生,引起

disturbance /dɪˈstɜːbəns/　n. actions that make you stop what you are doing, or that upset the normal state that sth. is in; the act of disturbing sb./sth. or the fact of being disturbed (受)打扰;干扰;妨碍

encounter /ɪnˈkaʊntə(r)/　v. to meet sb., or discover or experience sth., especially sb./sth. new, unusual or unexpected 偶然碰到;意外地遇见

　　　　　　　　　　　n. a meeting, especially one that is sudden, unexpected 相遇,邂逅

formidable /fəˈmɪdəbl/　adj. if people, things or situations are formidable, you feel fear and or respect for them, because they are impressive or powerful, or because they seem very difficult 可怕的,令人敬畏的,难对付的

flourish /ˈflʌrɪʃ/　v. to develop quickly and be successful or common; to grow well; to be healthy and happy 繁荣,昌盛,兴旺;茁壮成长,健康幸福

submarine /ˌsʌbməˈriːn/　adj. existing or located under the sea 水下的,海底的

　　　　　　　　　　　n. ship that can travel underwater 潜艇

diminutive /dɪˈmɪnjətɪv/　adj. very small 极小的,特小的,微小的

circulate /ˈsɜːkjəleɪt/　v. when a liquid, gas, or air circulates or is circulated, it moves continuously around a place or system; if a story, an idea, information, etc. circulates or if you circulate it, it spreads or it is passed from one person to another (液体或气体)环流,循环;传播,流传,散布

temperament /ˈtemprəmənt/　n. a person's or an animal's nature as shown in the way they behave or react to situations or people (人或动物的)气质,性情,性格,禀性

intimidate /ɪnˈtɪmɪdeɪt/　v. to frighten or threaten sb. so that they will do what you want 恐吓,威胁

territory /ˈterətri/　n. land that is under the control of a particular country or ruler; an area that one person, group, animal, etc. considers as their own and defends against others who try to enter it 领土,版图,领地;(个人、群体、动物等占据的)领域,管区,地盘

complacent /kəmˈpleɪsnt/　adj. too satisfied with yourself or with a situation, so that you do not feel that any change is necessary; showing or feeling complacency 自满的,自鸣得意的;表现出自满的

coordinate /kəʊˈɔːdɪneɪt/　v. to organize the different parts of an activity and the people involved in it so that it works well 使协调,使相配合

deploy /dɪˈplɔɪ/　v. to move soldiers or weapons into a position where they are ready for military action 部署,调度(军队或武器)

fragility /frəˈdʒɪləti/   n. quality of being easily damaged or destroyed 脆弱，易碎性，虚弱
desperate /ˈdespərət/   adj. giving little hope of success; tried when everything else has failed 绝望的；孤注一掷的
submersible /səbˈmɜːsəbl/   adj. that can be used underwater 水下使用的
　　　　　　　　　　　　　n. a ship that can travel underwater (goes underwater for short periods) 可潜船，潜水器
hair-raising /ˈheəˌreɪzɪŋ/   adj. extremely frightening but often exciting 使人毛发直立(惊险)的
footage /ˈfʊtɪdʒ/   n. part of a movie showing a particular event (影片中的)连续镜头，片段
thrive /θraɪv/   v. to become, and continue to be successful, strong, healthy, etc. 兴旺发达，繁荣，蓬勃发展，旺盛，茁壮成长

☞ **4. Character description**

Direction：*Describe the main characters (creatures) by using at least 5 adjectives in this documentary with the reference of the words you have learned, and find examples in the movie to support your ideas (Table 10.1).*

Table 10.1　Creatures from *Blue Planet* II (Episode 1)

Creatures	Adjectives	Examples
Bottlenose Dolphin (宽吻海豚)		
Tusk Fish(猪齿鱼)		
Trevally(鲹)		
False Killer Whale (伪虎鲸)		
Kobudai(金黄突额隆头鱼)		
Orca(虎鲸)		

Section II In-class Tasks

☞ **1. Workshop**

Direction：*Discuss the following questions with your classmates, and use the following sentence structures if it is possible.*

Sentence structures for causes & effect
- *Consequently …*

- The most likely reason for _____ was …
- The most significant cause of _____ was _____ because …
- One piece of evidence that supports my decisions is …
- This event occurred due to …
- One effect of _____ was …
- The video indicates that _____ was important to _____ because …

(1) What is the current condition of our oceans?

(2) What animal is challenging our understanding of fish intelligence? Why?

(3) How do seaweeds and sea grasses benefit mankind?

(4) What draws in rare visitors to New Zealand every spring? What are these rare animals?

(5) How does an orca hunt for fish?

(6) What causes global warming according to the documentary?

☞ 2. Cloze

Direction: *Fill in the gaps in the following passages taken from the movie with the words or phrases given below.*

■ Passage 1

playfulness	deliberately	character	ought to	youngsters
appreciate	reluctant	properties	extremely	sheer
infection	behave	watching	protect	covered

Bottlenose dolphins, they are ___1___ intelligent. And with this intelligence comes ___2___. They surf. And as far as we can tell, they do so for the ___3___ joy of it. But to properly ___4___ their true ___5___, you have to travel with them, into their world. A pod of bottlenose dolphins is visiting a coral reef in the Red Sea. For the ___6___, there are things to be learned here. The adults lead a calf to a particular bush-like coral, called a Gorgonian. And here, the adults ___7___ rather strangely. They ___8___ rub themselves through the fans. Their calf seems ___9___ to do so.

By ___10___ his elders, he may be realizing that this is something he ___11___ do. Gorgonian fans, in fact, are ___12___ with mucus, which can have anti-inflammatory and antimicrobial ___13___. So maybe the adult dolphins are doing this to ___14___ themselves from ___15___.

■ Passage 2

shore	reward	shoot	massive	spotted
close	anticipated	slow-motion	horizon	hair-raising
detailed	20-foot	prospect	imagined	high-speed

This year, the waves are bigger than anyone had ___1___. A daunting ___2___ for surf cameraman Chris Bryan. "Yeah, I'm feeling pretty nervous. It's a big swell out there, a really big swell, like, there is ___3___ waves out there and … Yeah, this will probably be the biggest seas I think I've ever been out in. No risks, no ___4___, I guess." Chris has a ___5___ camera to ___6___ super ___7___ action in the waves. The challenge is to get as ___8___ to the wave-riding dolphins as possible. The good news is that the dolphins have been ___9___ on the ___10___. "They said this was going to be the biggest swell of the year. Hey, I've never seen anything like this. This is much bigger than I have possibly ___11___." In these waves, the only way to get out to the dolphins is with a jet-ski. "That's got to be enough of a challenge for them just to kind of weave their way out." At last, the driver's ___12___ knowledge gets them safely through the ___13___ breakers. But the dolphins are nowhere to be seen. Leaving the crew to face the ___14___ task of getting back to ___15___.

☞ 3. Story retelling

Direction: *Study the information in Reference 1 on expository documentary of this unit, and then retell the story of* Blue Planet Ⅱ (Episode 1) *by using specific details to support your ideas* (*Table 10.2*).

Table 10.2 Expository Documentary Structure of *Blue Planet* Ⅱ (Episode 1)

Expository Documentary Structure	*Blue Planet* Ⅱ (Episode 1)
Cause & Effect: Ideas, events in time or facts are presented as causes of the resulting effects or facts that happen as a result of an event.	
Compare & Contrast: Information is presented by detailing how two or more events, concepts, theories, or things are alike and different.	
Description: A topic is described by listing characteristics, features, attributes, and examples.	
Problem & Solution: A problem and one or more solutions to the problem are outlined.	
Sequence: Items or events are listed in numerical or chronological sequence, either explicitly/implied.	

4. Sentence rearrangement

Direction: *Put the following sentences into the chronological order based on the story of Blue Planet* Ⅱ *(Episode 1) (Table 10.3).*

Table 10.3　Sentences from *Blue Planet* Ⅱ (Episode 1)

Orders	Sentences
	Oceans cover 70% of the surface of our planet, and yet, they are still the least explored.
	The oceans hold 97% of all the water in the world. As the sun warms their surface, water evaporates.
	This formidable hunting party now harvests the riches that come with New Zealand's summer.
	This sudden warming most likely a consequence of human activity is having a profound impact on its wildlife.
	Solving these problems together helps create a bond so strong that the mother will stay in contact with her young for the rest of her life.
	There is a fish here that, amazingly, has a brain capable of calculating the air speed, altitude and trajectory of a bird.
	But the sea is an unpredictable and dangerous place to work.
	The density of the animals on tropical reefs makes the competition inevitable and extreme.
	As we understand more out the complexities of the lives of sea creatures, so we begin to appreciate the fragility of their home.
	Explore our final frontier, the deep.

Section III　English Chat Task

Direction: *Discuss the themes of this video and organize your words on the specific themes (Table 10.4).*

Table 10.4　Themes of *Blue Planet* Ⅱ (Episode 1)

Themes	Questions about Themes	Answers (Key Words for Each Question)
Ocean	• What do you know about the oceans? • How do we feel about the oceans?	

continued

Themes	Questions about Themes	Answers (Key Words for Each Question)
Marine creatures	• What creatures are mentioned in the first episode? • Among all the creatures mentioned, which one do you like most? Why?	
Storm	• There are many ocean-related natural disasters. What are they? • How does storm come into being and how much energy could a large storm release?	
Intelligence of marine creatures	• Do you think creatures in the oceans are intelligent? Can you give examples from the documentary?	
Filming of the documentary	• What do you think of this documentary? • What is the primary purpose of it? • According to the documentary, what makes the filming of this documentary possible?	

Section IV   EANLIC Party Tasks

☞ **1. Give a presentation on the theme of *Blue Planet* II (Episode 1)**

☞ **2. Shadowing exercise**

Direction: *Prepare this part in groups before class. Please repeat what you hear from the video for at least 5 minutes. While doing this, you should make sure that you can catch up with the video, and then try to imitate the narrator's pronunciation and intonation.*

☞ **3. Debate**

Direction: *Study the debate information in Reference 2 of this unit, and then rebut your debate more effectively.*

(1) Is social and economic development more important than environmental protection nowadays?

For: Social and economic development is more important than environmental protection.

Against: Environmental protection is more important than social and economic development.

(2) Are individuals more important than governments in protecting the environment?

For: Individuals are more important in protecting the environment.

Against: Governments are more important in protecting the environment.

Section V After-class Tasks

☞ 1. Mindmap drawing

Direction: *Read Reference 1 of this unit, and then draw a mindmap of* Blue Planet Ⅱ *(Episode 1).*

☞ 2. Movie review

Direction: *Enjoy reading the information of Reference 3 and the movie review sample of* Wild China. *Scan the QR code for the movie review sample and addresses attached for your further study.*

References

☞ 1. Expository documentary

An expository documentary is one that has a commentator who talks over both videos and pictures to explain a specific story. Usually, it is an authoritative commentary, and vehemently proposes a particular point of view or argument.

It is informative, instructional, and educative. Also, it is not only rhetorical but also persuasive. It ensures that the viewer interprets the comments, images, and videos in a certain way.

It is also objective. It has various modes, different forms of the organization and several techniques used by the speaker to shape not only the voice but also the feelings. The documentary shows evidence supporting the argument or point of view.

In most cases, there are interviews of witnesses giving testimonies. The witnesses' role is to contribute the evidence. However, they don't determine the tone or perspective. As much as the images are not necessary, they play a huge role in strengthening the argument. Other than informing and persuading, an expository documentary also arouses curiosity. It evokes and gratifies one's curiosity to know more about what the narrator is talking about. The following mindmap provides you with more information about it.

Expository documentary

Definition
It is one that has a commentator who talks over both videos and pictures to explain a specific story. Usually, it is an authoritative commentary, and proposes a particular point of view or argument.

Key features
- It is objective, informative, instructional, persuasive and educative.
  - It ensures that the viewer interprets the comments, images, and videos in a certain way.
- It bases on facts.
  - It is fact-based, and these facts are mainly derived from interviews of people giving testimonies.
- It supports with narration.
  - It is a crucial part of any expository documentary, for it provides evidence and information.
- It includes evidentiary editing.
  - It is supported by evidentiary editing like subtitles and graphic elements.
- It has a final conclusion.

Format
It usually follows one of five formats: cause and effect, compare and contrast, description, problem and solution, and sequence.

Expository documentary

Cause & Effect
Ideas, events in time or facts are presented as causes of the resulting effects or facts that happen as a result of an event.

Compare & Contrast
Information is presented by detailing how two or more events, concepts, theories, or things are alike and different.

Description
A topic is described by listing characteristics, features, attributes, and examples.

Problem & Solution
A problem and one or more solutions to the problem are outlined.

Sequence
Items or events are listed in numerical or chronological sequence, either explicitly/implied.

☞ 2. How to rebut better?

Rebuttals are the most exciting part of the debate because they are the least predictable. In your rebuttal, you will respond to the arguments your opponent has made in the debate. You'll need to refute all of their arguments thoroughly. While you'll be developing your rebuttal during the actual debate, you can prepare yourself to write a better rebuttal by knowing your argument, anticipating possible counter-arguments, and familiarizing yourself with strategies that will allow you to break down your opponent's points. You can learn the tips on how to rebut better from the following information.

Tips on better rebuttals

- **Know your argument**
  - You need to have a solid grasp of the topic, your stance on the topic, the reasons that support that stance, and the evidence that you will use to support those reasons.

- **Write out your 3 or 4 main arguments**
  - You can highlight and outline your main arguments in your written case, since your opponent will be attacking your arguments at once.

- **Keep track of the arguments made by both you and your opponent**
  - Take good notes during the debate so that you remember to address new arguments that are brought up and don't accidentally forget about arguments that you've already made.

- **Make an outline of your arguments to refer to as you rebut**
  - Put your arguments into an outline that you can refer to in order to make sure all of your points are addressed in your rebuttal.

- **Restate your position**
  - Remind the judge what your argument is, positioning it as the clear better choice over your opponent. Choose your words carefully so that your argument appears to be the most reasonable choice.

- **Explain the reasons why your argument is the best**
  - Link your argument back to the topic, and provide evidence to back it up.

- **Give a concluding statement urging the judge to choose your argument**
  - Summarize your arguments and the voting issues briefly, and then urge the judge to vote for you.

☞ 3. Tips for writing a documentary review

Naturally, every documentary review is different. But there are a few golden rules that'll ensure your writing is reasonable.

Tips for writing a documentary review

Use the active voice and the present tense

This will make your writing feel more alive, immersing the readers in the story. Tell the readers what they'll see and hear on the screen as the documentary unfolds, from the beginning to the end.

Be specific

Use vivid, colorful language and avoid generic phrases or clichés. Your writing needs to describe situations, locations and characters in precise detail to make the story jump off the page.

Use nontechnical language

Make sure you don't use any inside film-making terms that the average readers won't understand. Not everyone reading your documentary review will be a cinematic expert or screenwriting buff.

Only describe what's seen and heard on camera

Don't include characters' desires, emotions or inner thoughts. And definitely don't describe camera directions.

Unit 11

Green Book

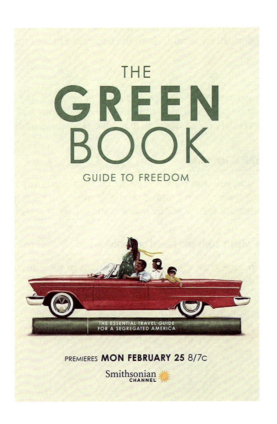

Unit Objectives:

1. Speaking skills:
   - Learn to accurately retell the story in this movie using the three-act story structure.
   - Develop skills to structure persuasive arguments for a debate.
2. Emotional objectives:
   - Cultivate students' love for diverse and rich cultures.
   - Encourage students' sense of responsibility for protecting and preserving cultural diversity, particularly within ethnic minority cultures.
   - Foster a sense of national unity, promoting the idea that all ethnic groups are united together "like the seeds of a pomegranate".

Section I Pre-class Tasks

The students are supposed to watch the movie of *Green Book* for at least 2 or 3 times ahead of the class, the first time for general understanding of the movie, and the second and third times for more detailed understanding and learning of English language, and then complete the following tasks before the class time.

☞ 1. Classic movie lines

Direction: *Read and recite the following lines from the movie.*

(1) You never win with violence! You only win when you maintain your dignity.
(2) It takes courage to change people's hearts.
(3) Ask not your country what you could do for it; ask what you do for yourself.

☞ 2. Background knowledge

Direction: *Go through the passage and prepare to share the information in class.*

The film is adapted from a true story. It tells the story between a well-known pianist and his driver. In 1962, in New York, Tony needs a new job badly, because the club he works in closes up for remodeling. He is recommended by a friend to go to an interview of a famous pianist looking for a driver and bodyguard. It is Don Shirley, a prestigious classical and jazz pianist, and descent of Jamaican immigrants, who is looking for a driver and bodyguard to accompany him on a tour through the Midwest and the Deep South.

Tony is racist. He is initially interested in the job, but during the interview, Tony shows that he harbors some racist feelings. The following day, Don calls to speak to his wife, Dolores and asks her permission to take Tony on the road with him. She approves on one condition that Tony writes her letters on the road.

Tony starts his job, equipped with a nice car and the "Green Book", which is a guidebook for safe restaurants and motels for black people in the segregated South. On the road, Tony and Don clash with each other, as Tony is rough around the edges and loud, whereas Don is more refined. One day, when he waits for Don, hearing his playing, Tony is impressed by his talent. Tony introduces Don to contemporary black culture. Don helps Tony write more romantic letters to Dolores and teaches him stealing is wrong. In the south, they must stay in separate hotels based on their race. One night, Tony saves Don from some white racists by bluffing. They encounter racial discrimination along the journey, and Don is discriminated. They've been put into prison and released with the help of the Attorney General, Robert Kennedy.

On the last night of the tour, Don refuses to play because of being discriminated by the hosts. He and Tony go to a black club instead, where his play wins much acclaim.

Tony and Don begin their drive back to New York, hoping to make it by Christmas Eve. The weather is really bad, with a lot of snow. Tony is too tried and sleepy to drive back to New York on time. He goes asleep and Don drives them the rest of the way to Tony's apartment. He wakes Tony up and encourages him to go home. Tony invites him to come upstairs with him but he refuses. But finally, Tony goes to Tony's. While most of the family is a little confused, Dolores joyously welcomes him and thanks him for helping Tony with his letters.

☞ 3. Vocabulary

Direction：*Learn these new words from this movie and try to use them at EANLIC night.*

sanitation /ˌsænɪˈteɪʃn/ *n.* the process of keeping places clean and healthy, especially by providing a sewage system and a clean water supply 公共卫生，环境卫生

foreman /ˈfɔːmən/ *n.* a person, especially a man, in charge of a group of workers 领班

chauffeur /ˈʃəʊfə(r)/ *n.* a man or a woman who is employed to look after their car and drive them around in it（富人或要人的）私人司机

availability /əˌveɪləˈbɪləti/ *n.* if something you want or need is available, you can find it or obtain it 能找到的，可获得的

itinerary /aɪˈtɪnərəri/ *n.* a plan of a journey, including the route and the places that you will visit 路线，旅程

trio /ˈtriːəʊ/ *n.* a musical composition for three performers 三重奏

sneak /sniːk/ *n.* someone who prowls or sneaks about; usually with unlawful intentions 鬼鬼祟祟的人；告密的人

bastard /ˈbɑːstəd/ *n.* an insulting word which some people use about a person, especially a man, who has behaved very badly 坏蛋，混蛋

absurd /əbˈsɜːd/ *adj.* completely ridiculous; not logical and sensible 荒谬的，荒唐的；不合理的

orphan /ˈɔːfn/ *n.* a child who has lost both parents 孤儿

campfire /ˈkæmpfaɪə(r)/ *n.* a fire that you light out of doors when you are camping 营火，篝火

intonation /ˌɪntəˈneɪʃn/ *n.* rise and fall of the voice pitch 语调，声调

inflection /ɪnˈflekʃn/ *n.* an inflection in someone's voice is a change in its tone or pitch as they are speaking 变音，转调

debut /ˈdeɪbjuː/ *n.* the first public appearance of a performer or sports player 首次登台，初次露面

terrific /təˈrɪfɪk/ *adj.* extraordinarily good, used especially as intensifiers 极好的，非常棒的，了不起的

insult /ɪnˈsʌlt/ *v.* to say or do sth. that offends sb. 侮辱，辱骂

grease /griːs/ *n.* thick fatty oil 动物油脂，油膏

enunciate /ɪˈnʌnsieɪt/ *v.* to say or pronounce words clearly 清楚地念(字),清晰地发(音)

rehearse /rɪˈhɜːs/ *v.* to practise or make peole practise a play, piece of music, etc. in preparation for a public performance 排练,演练,预演(戏剧、舞蹈或音乐作品)

expounding /ɪkˈspaʊndɪŋ/ *n.* if you expound an idea or opinion, you give a clear and detailed explanation of it 详述,阐述,详细说明

dice /daɪs/ *n.* small cubes with 1 to 6 spots on the faces; a game played with dice 骰子,掷骰游戏

make-up /ˈmeɪkʌp/ *n.* substances used especially by women to make their faces look more attractive or used by actors to change their appearances 化妆品

flagrant /ˈfleɪɡrənt/ *adj.* shocking because it is done in a very obvious way and shows no respect for people, laws, etc. 骇人听闻的,罪恶昭彰的,公然的

mattress /ˈmætrəs/ *n.* the large, flat object which is put on a bed to make it comfortable to sleep on 床垫

nigger /ˈnɪɡə(r)/ *n.* an extremely offensive word for a black person 黑人,黑鬼(蔑称);下层人

assumption /əˈsʌmpʃn/ *n.* a belief or feeling that something is true or will happen, although there is no proof 假设,臆断

utensil /juːˈtensl/ *n.* a tool that is used in the house 器皿,(家庭)用具

exception /ɪkˈsepʃn/ *n.* a particular thing, person, or situation that is not included in a general statement, judgment, or rule 例外,除外

hypnotize /ˈhɪpnətaɪz/ *v.* to produce a state of hypnosis in sb. 对……施催眠术,使进入催眠状态

☞ 4. Character description

Direction: *Describe the main characters by using at least 5 adjectives in this movie with the reference of the words you have learned, and find examples in the movie to support your ideas (Table 11.1).*

Table 11.1 Main Characters in *Green Book*

Main Characters	Adjectives	Examples
Dr. Shirley		
Tony Lip		

Section II In-class Tasks

☞ 1. Workshop

Direction: *Discuss the questions with your classmates, and use the following sentence* structures *if it is possible*.

Sentence structures

- *The movie explicitly states ...*
- *The movie reveals ...*
- *This movie reminds me of ... because ...*
- *One thing I don't understand about this movie is ...*
- *I share your perspective ...*
- *I have a different viewpoint ...*

(1) What do you like or dislike about *Green Book*?

(2) What is the function of the real green book?

(3) What's your impression on Doctor Shirley?

(4) What's your impression on Tony Lip?

(5) How do you think of Tony Lip's wife?

(6) Was there something you didn't understand about the movie? What was that?

2. Cloze

Direction: *Fill in the gaps in the following passages taken from the movie with the words or phrases given below.*

■ **Passage 1**

spirit	to rest of my life	reminded	easiest	aware	distance
Falling	experiences	met	meaningless	alive	plains

When I think of you, I'm ___1___ of the beautiful ___2___ of Iowa. The ___3___ between us is breaking my ___4___. My time and ___5___ without you are ___6___ to me. ___7___ in love with you was the ___8___ thing I have ever done. And every day I am ___9___, I'm ___10___ of this. I love you the day I ___11___ you. I love you today. And I will love you ___12___.

■ **Passage 2**

explain	bursts with	fairytale	concert	leafy
shed	count	hold inside	dusted with	faded to
family	getting colder	in my arms	beautiful	shows

The trees have ___1___ their ___2___ clothing and their colors have ___3___ grays and browns, but my heart ___4___ reds and blues and greens from the love I ___5___ for you ... It's ___6___ as we travel, but the country is still ___7___. I saw millions of trees, all ___8___ snow, just like out of a ___9___ ... We've only a few more ___10___ before our Christmas ___11___ in Birmingham, Alabama on the 23rd. I'm just saying, we're a ___12___ . I would ___13___ the hours, minutes, and seconds until you are ___14___ . I love and miss you more than I can ___15___ .

☞ 3. Story retelling

Direction: *Study the information in Reference 1 on the three-act story structure of this unit, and then retell the story of* Green Book *by using specific details to support your ideas (Table 11.2).*

Table 11.2　The Three-Act Story Sturcture of *Green Book*

The Three-Act Story Structure	Green Book
Act 1: The Setup	
Act 2: The Conflict	
Act 3: The Climax	

☞ 4. Sentence rearrangement

Direction: *Put the following sentences into the chronological order based on the story of* Green Book *(Table 11.3).*

Table 11.3　Sentences from *Green Book*

Orders	Sentences
	I'm not a doctor. I'm a musician, and I'm on my way to a music tour of the southern United States.
	If I'm not black enough, and if I'm not white enough, and if I'm not man enough, then tell me, what am I?
	Mr. Villanueva, you have to talk sense to Mr. Shirley. Please make him understand we're not insulting him personally. This is just the way things are done down here.
	You'd better be home for Christmas or don't come home at all.
	And rich white people pay me to play the piano for them, because it makes them feel cultured.
	I got no problem being on a road with you.

continued

Orders	Sentences
	How did he manage to shake hands with them with a smile? Because it takes courage to get rid of stereotypes.
	My father used to say, whatever you do, do it a hundred percent. When you eat, eat like it's your last meal.
	Falling in love with you is the easiest thing I've ever done.
	And I know you're the kind of man who honors a contract!

Section III English Chat Task

Direction: *Discuss the themes of this movie and organize your words on the specific themes (Table 11.4).*

Table 11.4 Themes of *Green Book*

Themes	Questions about Themes	Answers (Key Words for Each Question)
Racial discrimination	• How serious is racial discrimination in the 1960s in the US? • Could you list some examples in the movie?	
Dignity	• How do both characters win their own dignity?	
Loneliness	• Does Dr. Shirley feel lonely? And give your reasons.	
Society and class	• What is Dr. Shirley's social role in the movie? • What is Tony's social class in the movie? • What is the strongest emotion that you feel when watching the movie?	

Section IV EANLIC Party Tasks

☞ **1. Give a presentation on the theme of *Green Book***

☞ 2. Role-play

Direction: *Prepare this part in groups before class, and then do the role-play in class. Scan the QR code for role-play scripts.*

(1) Tony attends an interview with Dr. Shirley.
(2) Dr. Shirley is refused entry into the whites-only dining room of the country club venue where he has been hired to perform.

☞ 3. Debate

Direction: *Study the debate information in Reference 2 of this unit, and then structure your debate with persuasive arguments.*

(1) Can you win with violence?
   For: You can win with violence.
   Against: You can never win with violence.
(2) Does cultural background have an impact on one's personality?
   For: Cultural background has an effect on one's personality.
   Against: Cultural background does not have an effect on one's personality.

Section V After-class Tasks

☞ 1. Mindmap drawing

Direction: *Read Reference 1 of this unit once again, and then draw a mindmap on* Green Book.

☞ 2. Movie review

Direction: *Enjoy reading the movie review sample in Unit 12. Scan the QR code for the movie review sample and addresses attached for your further study.*

References

☞ 1. The three-act story structure

The three-act story structure is a narrative arc composed of three acts forming a beginning, middle, and end. It is perhaps the most common technique in the English-speaking world for plotting stories. It is a model used in narrative fiction that divides a story into three parts (or acts), often called the setup, the conflict, and the climax. The first act introduces the central characters and conflicts; the second act explores the way the central characters react to these conflicts; and the third act reveals the consequence of these reactions and choices. You can learn more about it from the following mindmap.

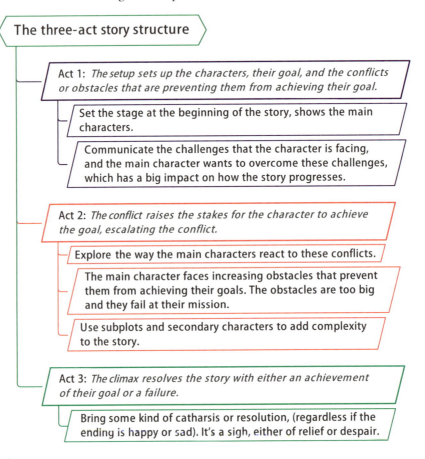

☞ 2. How to structure an argument in debate?

An argument is an act of expressing a point of view on a subject and supporting that view using evidence such as research, statistics and examples. You may choose to follow a particular structure when crafting your argument depending upon situational factors like the subject of it, your audience and the type of evidence you have access to. Regardless of these factors, though, there are a few fundamental steps you can take to structure an argument effectively. Here are five essential steps to follow when building an argument.

How to structure an argument in debate?

Introduce the problem
- Introduce the problem or issue at the center of your argument.
- Provide relevant background information that may enable your audience to understand your argument.
- Provide a basic outline of the evidence you plan to present.

Present your caim
- Offer your perspective on the issue.
- Present concise and direct claim that are easily intelligible by your audience.

Support your claim
- Provide evidence that supports your claim.
- Present examples, research, statistics, studies and other information that proves your claim and fosters a sense of validity.
- Focus on offering facts rather than anecdotal information.

Acknowledge the opposing side of the argument
- Acknowledge the opposing side of your argument after offering adequate evidence to support your claim.
- Explain why you disagree with counterclaims, disprove their validity or concede to their validity within certain contexts.
- Address opposing perspectives will help you maintain objectivity and add credibility to your argument overall.

Restate your claim
- Draw conclusions about your claim by restating it and briefly summarizing the evidence you presented.
- Present an appeal to the audience's emotions or perspective that can further persuade them.
- Explain how the issue personally affects your audience to demonstrate your argument's importance.

Unit 12

Forrest Gump

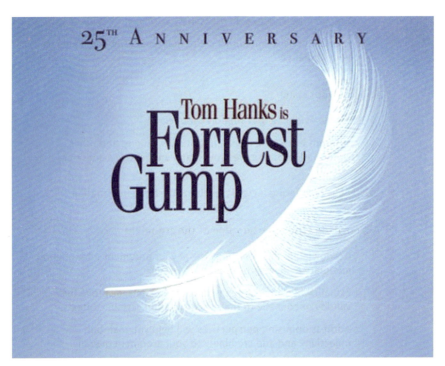

Unit Objectives:

1. Speaking skills:
   - Learn the In Medias Res structure to effectively retell the story in this movie.
   - Develop skills to conclude a persuasive debate with a strong conclusion.
2. Emotional objectives:
   - Cultivate students' courage to discover their potential and overcome challenges in real life situations.
   - Encourage students' persistence towards realizing their dreams.
   - Foster a sense of optimism in difficult situations, promoting a positive outlook on life.

Section I Pre-class Tasks

The students are supposed to watch the movie of *Forrest Gump* for at least 2 or 3 times ahead of the class, the first time for general understanding of the movie, and the second and third times for more detailed understanding and learning of English language, and then complete the following tasks before the class time.

1. Classic movie lines

Direction: *Read and recite the following lines from the movie.*

(1) Life is like a box of chocolates. You never know what you're gotta get.
(2) A promise is a promise.
(3) You've got to put the past behind you before you can move on.

2. Background knowledge

Direction: *Go through the passage and prepare to share the information in class.*

Beginning with a white drifting feather in the air, the film tells the story of Forrest Gump, an amiable "idiot" born in the 1950s, with an I.Q. of 75. His mother bribes the school principle and gets him into a public school. On his first day to school, he meets Jenny, later his friend and loved one, on the school bus. The two become good friends like peas and carrots. One day, Forrest discovers his talent for running while being encouraged by Jenny to run away from the bullies. Forrest falls in love with Jenny. He gets admission to college for his talent for running and becomes a football star.

Upon graduation, he is recruited to the US army and sent to fight the Vietnam War. On the way to the military camp, he meets another friend, Bubba, an African American, who has always been dreaming to start a shrimping business. Forrest serves under Lieutenant Dan, a proud man from a military family. Forrest perfectly fits into the army. One day, while patrolling, the team engages in a fight with the enemy. Forrest manages to save Lieutenant Dan and some other soldiers, while Bubba dies in his arms. Forrest gets shot on his bottom. The wounded are sent to a military hospital. So do Forrest and Lieutenant Dan. In the hospital, Forrest learns to play ping-pong and discovers his talent for playing it.

After retiring from the army, Forrest is selected to represent the USA in China and plays ping-pong with a Chinese player. Going back home, he becomes a well-know person and earns money from sponsorship of ping-pong paddles. Forrest spends the money in buying a shrimping boat and sets up a shrimping business, fulfilling his promise to Bubba of going in for shrimping business. Lieutenant Dan keeps his promise of being Forrest's first mate if he should be a captain. They make a lot of money after a storm sinks other shrimping boats. Lieutenant Dan invests in Apple, and Forrest becomes a billionaire.

Jenny comes back and stays with Forrest for some time, but she goes away again. One day, for no particular reason, Forrest starts his epic run and he ends his running one day when he thinks he would like to go home. He inspires a lot of people during his running.

Back at home in Alabama, one day he gets a letter from Jenny asking him to meet her. Forrest finds he has a son with Jenny. They go back to Alabama together, and they hold a wedding ceremony. Jenny dies of a deadly virus. Forrest sends little Forrest to go to school. A white feather is drifting in the air, and another circle of life begins.

☞ **3. Vocabulary**

Direction：*Learn these new words and expression(s) from this movie and try to use them at EANLIC night.*

bunch /bʌntʃ/ *n.* a number of things of the same type which are growing or fastened together 串,束,扎

brace /breɪs/ *n.* a device that holds things firmly together or holds and supports them in position 箍子,夹子,支架

principal /ˈprɪnsəpl/ *n.* (AmE) head teacher, a teacher who is in charge of a school 校长

case /keɪs/ *n.* a container or covering used to protect or store things; a container with its contents or the amount that it contains 容器,箱,盒,套,罩;容器及内装物;(容器的)容量

sample /ˈsɑːmpl/ *n.* a small amount or example of sth. that can be looked at or tried to see what it is like (作为标准或代表的)样品,货样

swing /swɪŋ/ *v.* to move backwards or forwards or from side to side while hanging from a fixed point; to make sth. do this (使)摆动,摇摆,摇荡

dandy /ˈdændi/ *adj.* very good 好的,棒的,正好的

crooked /ˈkrʊkɪd/ *adj.* not in a straight line, bent or twisted 不直的,弯曲的,扭曲的

dangle /ˈdæŋgl/ *v.* to hang or swing freely 悬垂,悬挂,悬荡,悬摆

miracle /ˈmɪrəkl/ *n.* a lucky thing that happens that you did not expect or think was possible 奇迹,不平凡的事

retarded /rɪˈtɑːdɪd/ *adj.* less developed mentally than is normal for a particular age 智力迟钝的,智力发育迟缓的

plain /pleɪn/ *adv.* used to emphasize how bad, stupid, etc. sth. is (用于强调)简直,绝对地

mysterious /mɪˈstɪəriəs/ *adj.* difficult to understand or explain; strange 神秘的,不易解释的;奇怪的

scared /skeəd/ *adj.* frightened of sth. or afraid that sth. bad might happen 恐惧的

chase /tʃeɪs/ *v.* to run, drive, etc. after sb./sth. in order to catch them 追赶,追逐,追捕

dizzy /ˈdɪzi/ *adj.* feeling as if everything is spinning around you and that you are not able to balance 头晕目眩的,眩晕的

sole /səʊl/ *adj.* only; single 仅有的；唯一的

disassemble /ˌdɪsəˈsembl/ *v.* to take apart a machine or structure so that it is in separate pieces 拆卸，拆开

rescue /ˈreskjuː/ *v.* to save sb./sth. from a dangerous or harmful situation 营救，援救，抢救

salute /səˈluːt/ *v.* to touch the side of your head with the fingers of your right hand to show respect, especially in the armed forces （尤指军队中）敬礼

quit /kwɪt/ *v.* to stop doing sth. 停止，戒掉

lean /liːn/ *v.* to rest on or against sth. for support 倚靠，靠在，靠置

grab /græb/ *v.* to take or hold sb./sth. with your hand suddenly, firmly or roughly 抓住，攫取

destiny /ˈdestəni/ *n.* what happens to sb. or what will happen to them in the future, especially things that they cannot change or avoid 命运，天命，天数

cripple /ˈkrɪpl/ *n.* a person who is unable to walk or move normally because of a disease or injury 伤残人，残疾人，跛子，瘸子

freak /friːk/ *n.* a person, an animal, a plant or a thing that is not physically normal（指人、动植物和东西）畸形

cheat /tʃiːt/ *v.* to trick sb. or make them believe sth. is not true 欺骗，蒙骗

candid /ˈkændɪd/ *adj.* saying what you think openly and honestly; not hiding your thoughts 坦率的，坦诚的，直言不讳的

escalation /ˌeskəˈleɪʃn/ *n.* an increase in extent, volume, number, amount, intensity, or scope 升级，增加；扩大

Expression(s)

sneak out leave furtively and stealthily 偷偷溜出去，偷偷溜走

☞ 4. Character description

Direction: *Describe the main characters by using at least 5 adjectives in this movie with the reference of the words you have learned, and find examples in the movie to support your ideas (Table 12.1).*

Table 12.1 Main Characters in *Forrest Gump*

Main Characters	Adjectives	Examples
Forrest Gump		
Lieutenant Dan		
Jenny		
Mrs. Gump		
Bubba		

Section II In-class Tasks

☞ 1. Workshop

Direction: *Discuss the questions with your classmates, and use the following sentence structures if it is possible.*

Sentence structures for opinions

- The fact is ...
- Without a doubt ...
- Regardless of popular opinion ...
- It's my honest belief ...
- The facts are conclusive ...

(1) What do you like or dislike about Forrest Gump?

(2) Forrest receives the Congressional Medal of Honor. What does he receive it for?

(3) What is the significance of the feather?

(4) What are the differences between Forrest Gump and Jenny?

(5) What are the differences between Forrest Gump and Dan?

(6) Why does Forrest fit well in the army?

(7) How does Mrs. Gump explain death to Forrest?

(8) Why is Dan very angry about being saved by Forrest?

☞ 2. Cloze

Direction: *Fill in the gaps in the following passages taken from the movie with the words or phrases given below.*

■ **Passage 1**

brushes	combs	miss	destiny	right
placed	proud	breeze	life	smart
fish	floating	start school	bulldozed	supposed

You died on a Saturday morning. And I had you ___1___ here under our tree. And I had that house of your father's ___2___ to the ground. Mama always said dying was a part of ___3___. I sure wish it wasn't. Little Forrest, he's doing just fine. About to ___4___ again soon. I make his breakfast, lunch, and dinner every day. I make sure he ___5___ his hair and ___6___ his teeth every day. Teaching him how to play ping-pong. He's really good. We ___7___ a lot. And every night, we read a book. He's so ___8___, Jenny. You'd be so ___9___ of him. I am. He, uh, wrote a letter, and he says I can't read it. I'm not ___10___ to, so I'll just leave it here for you. Jenny, I don't know if mama was ___11___ or if, if it's Lieutenant Dan. I don't know if we each have a ___12___, or if we're all just

___13___ around accidental-like on a ___14___, but I, I think maybe it's both. Maybe both are happening at the same time. I ___15___ you, Jenny. If there's anything you need, I won't be far away.

■ **Passage 2**

| questions | angel | read | beautiful | special | sit out | conversation |
| swing | only | talked | next to | stars | From that day on |

I hadn't seen anything so ___1___ in my life. She was like an ___2___. I just sat ___3___ her on that bus and had a ___4___ all the way to school. Next to mama no one ever ___5___ to me or asked me ___6___. ___7___ we were always together. Jenny, she helped me learn how to ___8___ and I showed her how to ___9___. Sometimes we'd just ___10___ and wait for the ___11___. For some reason Jenny never wanted to go home. She was my most ___12___ friend, my ___13___ friend.

☞ **3. Story retelling**

Direction: Study the information in Reference 1 on the In Medias Res of this unit, and then retell the story of Forrest Gump by using specific details to support your ideas (Table 12.2).

Table 12.2 The In Medias Res Steps of Forrest Gump

The In Medias Res Steps	Forrest Gump
Start by choosing a pivotal, emotional scene to serve as your In Medias Res opener.	
Develop a plan for how to present the backstory that precedes your main plot.	
Make sure your opening is crucial to your plot.	
Make readers curious about how events led up to this point.	
Check that you aren't info-dumping.	
Write an intriguing first line.	

☞ **4. Sentence rearrangement**

Direction: Put the following sentences into the chronological order based on the story of Forrest Gump (Table 12.3).

Table 12.3 Sentences from *Forrest Gump*

Orders	Sentences
	From that day on, if I was going somewhere, I was running!
	Mama said they'd take me anywhere. She said they were my magic shoes.
	Mama always had a way of explaining things so I could understand them.
	I'm not a smart man ... but I know what love is.
	It's my time. It's just my time. Oh, now, don't be afraid, sweetheart. Death is just a part of life, something we're all destined to do.
	The secret to this game is, no matter what happens, never, ever take your eye off the ball.
	If I'd known that was the last time I was gonna talk to Bubba, I would've thought of something better to say.
	Those must be comfortable shoes; I bet you could walk all day in shoes like those and not feel a thing.
	One day it started raining, and it didn't quit for four months. We been through every kind of rain there is.
	Now you wouldn't believe me if I told you, but I could run like the wind blows.

Section III English Chat Task

Direction: *Discuss the themes of this movie and organize your words on the specific themes (Table 12.4).*

Table 12.4 Themes of *Forrest Gump*

Themes	Questions about Themes	Answers (Key Words for Each Question)
Non-action	• What is the symbolic meaning of the feather? • What does the chocolate symbolize?	
Non-judgment	• What is "good" and what is "bad" in the movie? Are they clear-cut in the movie? • What are the examples to show positive characteristics turn out to be disadvantageous? • What are the examples to illustrate negative events have positive consequences and positive events have negative consequences?	
Ignorance and blindness	• How does Forrest Gump's shrimping business thrive? • Does Forrest Gump lie about ping-pong paddles? Does he make money from lying?	

Themes	Questions about Themes	Answers (Key Words for Each Question)
Gump and America	• Does Forrest Gump bear any resemblance to America? If yes, what are these resemblances? • What American traditional ideals does Forrest Gump embody?	

continued

Section IV EANLIC Party Tasks

☞ 1. Give a presentation on the theme of *Forrest Gump*

☞ 2. Role-play

Direction: *Prepare this part before class, and then do the role-play in class. Scan the QR code for role-play scripts.*

(1) Mrs. Gump explains death to Forrest Gump.

(2) Forrest meets Jenny on the first day to school.

☞ 3. Debate

Direction: *Study the debate information in Reference 2 of this unit, and then conclude a persuasive debate with a strong conclusion.*

(1) Does Forrest's success result from perseverance or fortune?

   For: Forrest's success results from perseverance rather than fortune.

   Against: Forrest's success results from fortune rather than perseverance.

(2) Is success or happiness the most important in our life?

   For: Success is the most important in our life.

   Against: Happiness is more important than success.

Section V After-class Tasks

☞ 1. Mindmap drawing

Direction: *Read Reference 1 of this unit once again, and then draw a mindmap of* Forrest Gump.

☞ 2. Movie review

Direction: *Enjoy reading the following movie review sample of* Forrest Gump. *Scan the QR code for the movie review sample and addresses attached for*

your further study.

References

1. What is In Medias Res storytelling structure?

In Medias Res is a storytelling method in which a story begins in the middle or conclusion of the story rather than at the beginning. In Medias Res is a Latin phrase meaning "in the midst of things". It is a story that has to be set in the present, but can be told in the past or future. The story begins in the present, then jumps into the past or future, and ends in the present again, with the main character coming back to the present to resolve whatever conflict was created. Using In Medias Res in your story is as simple as following these six steps.

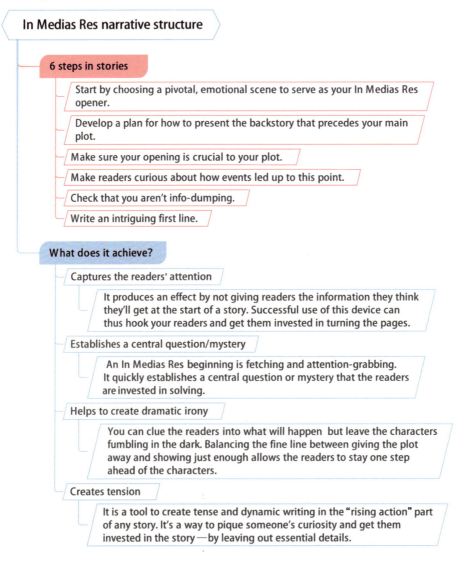

☞ 2. How to conclude a debate?

The conclusion is one of the most important parts of a debate speech. It should sum the points you have written in your debate, and the listeners or readers should feel as if they have gained the result of whatever you have written in the body of your debate. Writing a conclusion for a debate speech is the same as writing a conclusion for an essay.

When it comes to writing a debate essay, even good arguments can fall without a strong conclusion. Closing statements wrap up a debate's argument by connecting the evidence and the claim of the debate topic.

When finishing your debate speech, you have the opportunity to reiterate your most important points, conclude your arguments, give the judges something to think about, and ultimately deliver a logical conclusion.

How to conclude a debate?

Reference the introduction
- Going back to the opening statement adds cohesiveness to the overall speech.

Reuse the title
- Consider reiterating the title at the end of your debate speech.

Make it appropriate
- Make your speech precise, clear, and concise. This leaves the listeners satisfied.

Summarize the main points
- Summarize the main points of your debate speech in your conclusion. It is a good way to re-emphasize your main points.

Write a proper closing statement
- It is the culmination of the debate speech.
- It leaves the audience asking questions and pondering the ideas put across in the debate.
- It helps each side summarize their main arguments and stress critical points.
- It allows you to remind the judges of your opponents' shortcomings.

The aim is to persuasively convince your audience that your side has better arguments and leaves a lasting impression by ending with a powerful analogy.

Unit 13

The Sound of Music

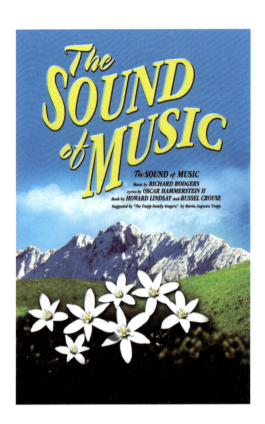

Unit Objectives:

1. Speaking skills:
   - Learn and effectively use Dan Harmon story circle structure to retell stories.
   - Improve skills in creating and delivering persuasive arguments in a debate, using provided tips to craft stronger debates.

2. Emotional objectives:
   - Encourage students' love for education, promoting a positive attitude towards learning and personal growth.
   - Foster a strong sense of family bond, helping students appreciate the value of close relationships with loved ones.

Section I Pre-class Tasks

The students are supposed to watch the movie of *The Sound of Music* for at least 2 or 3 times ahead of the class, the first time for general understanding of the movie, and the second and third times for more detailed understanding and learning of English language, and then complete the following tasks before the class time.

☞ 1. Classic movie lines

Direction: *Read and recite the following lines from the movie.*
(1) I must dream of the things I am seeking.
(2) The hills are alive with the sound of music.
(3) These walls were not built to shut out problems.

☞ 2. Background knowledge

Direction: *Go through the passage and prepare to share the information in class.*

The Sound of Music is based on the memoir of Maria von Trapp, *The Story of the Trapp Family Singers*. It was adapted as a musical film in 1965. The film tells the story of Maria, a sister in an abbey of Salzburg, Austria. She is sent to the von Trapp family to work as a governess to take care of the von Trapp children. Captain Georg von Trapp is a single father of 7 children. Because of his experience in the navy and the grief over the death of his wife, he is very strict with his children, treating them like marines. She wins the children's love with her gentleness and kindness. She makes play clothes out of curtains, takes them to the market, to picnic in the Alps and teaches them to sing. She fills their life with music and happiness.

One day Mr. von Trapp returns with Uncle Max and his girlfriend, a baroness, whom Mr. von Trapp is about to marry. He disapproves Maria's doing, but feels touched when the children sing to the baroness because he thinks Maria brings music back to the family. And he is also impressed when seeing the puppet show prepared by Maria and the children. Maria falls in love with Mr. von Trapp, but fearing for her love for him, she returns to the abbey.

After Maria leaves, the baroness tries to please the children but fails. The children feel sad about Maria's leaving. The news of their father marrying the baroness makes them more sorrowful. Being encouraged by the Reverend Mother, Maria returns to the von Trapp family. Mr. von Trapp falls in love with Maria, too. The baroness finds it impossible to win von Trapp's heart, so she quits. Maria and von Trapp finally get married.

During the honeymoon, Austria is taken by the Nazi. Mr. von Trapp refuses the Nazi offer of a position, and escapes with the help of Max and the nuns.

☞ 3. Vocabulary

Direction: *Learn these new words and expression(s) from this movie and try to use them at EANLIC night.*

abbey /ˈæbi/ *n.* a large church together with a group of buildings in which monks or nuns live or lived in the past 隐修院,(曾为大隐修院的)大教堂

barn /bɑːn/ *n.* a large farm building for storing grain or keeping animals in 谷仓,畜棚

adore /əˈdɔː(r)/ *v.* to love sb. very much 热爱,爱慕(某人)

beckon /ˈbekən/ *v.* to give sb. a signal using your finger or hand, especially to tell them to move nearer or to follow you 招手示意,举手召唤

summon /ˈsʌmən/ *v.* to order sb. to appear in court 传唤,传讯(出庭)

fragrant /ˈfreɪɡrənt/ *adj.* having a pleasant smell 香的,芳香的

postulant /ˈpɒstʃələnt/ *n.* a person who makes a request or application, esp. a candidate for admission to a religious order (圣职)申请人

governess /ˈɡʌvənəs/ *n.* (especially in the past) a woman employed to teach the children of a rich family in their home and to live with them (尤指旧时的)家庭女教师

sullen /ˈsʌlən/ *adj.* bad-tempered and not speaking, either on a particular occasion or because it is part of your character 面有愠色的,闷闷不乐的,郁郁寡欢的

rejoice /rɪˈdʒɔɪs/ *v.* to express great happiness about sth. 非常高兴,深感欣喜

grandeur /ˈɡrændʒə(r)/ *n.* the quality of being great and impressive in appearance 宏伟,壮丽,堂皇

butler /ˈbʌtlə(r)/ *n.* the main male servant in a large house 男管家

discipline /ˈdɪsəplɪn/ *n.* the practice of training people to obey rules and orders and punishing them if they do not; the controlled behaviour or situation that results from this training 训练,训导;纪律,风纪

drill /drɪl/ *v.* to teach sb. to do sth. by making them repeat it a lot of times 培训,训练

decorum /dɪˈkɔːrəm/ *n.* polite behavior that is appropriate in a social situation 礼貌得体,端庄稳重

whistle /ˈwɪsl/ *n.* a small metal or plastic tube that you blow to make a loud high sound, used to attract attention or as a signal 哨子

slam /slæm/ *v.* to shut, or to make sth. shut, with a lot of force, making a loud noise (使……)砰地关上

terrace /ˈterəs/ *n.* a flat, hard area, especially outside a house or restaurant, where you can sit, eat and enjoy the sun (尤指房屋或餐馆外的)露天平台,阳台

extensive /ɪkˈstensɪv/ *adj.* covering a large area; great in amount 广阔的,广大的;大量的

humiliate /hjuːˈmɪlieɪt/ *v.* to make sb. feel ashamed or stupid and lose the respect of other people 羞辱,使丧失尊严

incorrigible /ɪnˈkɒrɪdʒəbl/ *adj.* having bad habits which cannot be changed or improved 无法

改正的, 屡教不改的

parasol /ˈpærəsɒl/ *n.* a type of light umbrella that women in the past carried to protect themselves from the sun（旧时的）女用阳伞

toad /təʊd/ *n.* a small animal like a frog but with a drier and less smooth skin that lives on land but breeds in water（=is an amphibian）蟾蜍, 癞蛤蟆

pine cone /ˈpaɪn kəʊn/ *n.* the seed-producing cone of a pine tree 松果, 松球

indigestion /ˌɪndɪˈdʒestʃən/ *n.* pain caused by difficulty in digesting food 消化不良（症）

baroness /ˈbærənəs/ *n.* a woman who has the same rank as a baron. In Britain, baronesses use the title Lady or Baroness 女男爵（英国女男爵头衔为 Lady 或 Baroness）

decorate /ˈdekəreɪt/ *v.* to make sth. look more attractive by putting things on it 装饰, 装潢

canny /ˈkæni/ *adj.* intelligent, careful and showing good judgment, especially in business or politics（尤指在商业或政治方面）精明谨慎的, 老谋深算的

brink /brɪŋk/ *n.* the extreme edge of land, for example, at the top of a cliff or by a river（峭壁、河岸等的）边沿, 边缘

timid /ˈtɪmɪd/ *adj.* shy and nervous; not brave 羞怯的, 胆怯的; 缺乏勇气的

snowflake /ˈsnəʊfleɪk/ *n.* a small soft piece of frozen water that falls from the sky as snow 雪花, 雪片

eyelash /ˈaɪlæʃ/ *n.* one of the hairs growing on the edge of the eyelids 睫毛

repetitious /ˌrepəˈtɪʃəs/ *adj.* involving sth. that is often repeated 重复的, 反反复复的

puppet /ˈpʌpɪt/ *n.* a model of a person or an animal that can be made to move, for example, by pulling strings attached to parts of its body or by putting your hand inside it 木偶

defensive /dɪˈfensɪv/ *adj.* protecting sb./sth. against attack 防御的, 保护的, 保卫的

Expression(s)

Reverend Mother a title of respect used when talking to or about a Mother Superior（=the head of a female religious community）（对女修道院院长的尊称）可敬的修女

☞ 4. Character description

Direction: Describe the main characters by using at least 5 adjectives in this movie with the reference of the words you have learned, and find examples in the movie to support your ideas (Table 13.1).

Table 13.1 Main Characters in *The Sound of Music*

Main Characters	Adjectives	Examples
Maria		
Captain Georg von Trapp		
Elsa Schraeder		
Liesl von Trapp		

continued

Main Characters	Adjectives	Examples
Rolf Gruber		
Mother Abbess		
Max Detweiler		

Section II In-class Tasks

☞ 1. Workshop

Direction: Discuss the questions with your classmates, and use the following sentence structures if it is possible.

Sentence structures for expressing comparing & contrasting

- The similarities between _____ and _____ are …
- _____ and _____ are similar because …
- Another way that they are alike is …
- The differences between _____ and _____ are …
- _____ and _____ are different because …
- Another way that they are different is …

(1) Where did Maria live before she became a governess?
(2) How do you describe Captain von Trapp?
(3) Did the children like Maria at the beginning?
(4) Who do you like most among the children of the Trapp family?
(5) Can you describe one of the scenes that touch you?

☞ 2. Cloze

Direction: Fill in the gaps in the following dialogue and song taken from the movie with the words or phrases given below.

■ **Dialogue**

material	abbey	stare	trust	sea captain	No exceptions
twelfth	permit	governess	improvement	The poor	worldly clothes
two hours	drill	hat off	new dress	orderliness	maintain discipline

(While waiting, Maria enters a hall. It is such a magnificent hall that she can't help dancing. The captain appears.)

Captain: Why do you ___1___ at me that way?

Maria: Well, you don't look at all like a ___2___, sir.
Captain: I'm afraid you don't look much like a ___3___. Turn around, please.
Maria: What?
Captain: Turn ___4___. It's the dress. You have to put on another one before you meet the children.
Maria: But I don't have another one. When we enter the ___5___, our ___6___ are given to the poor.
Captain: What about this one?
Maria: ___7___ didn't want this one.
Captain: Hmm.
Maria: I would have made myself a ___8___, but there wasn't time. I can make my own clothes.
Captain: Well, I'll see that you get some ___9___. Today, if possible. Now, Fraulein … er …
Maria: Maria.
Captain: Fraulein Maria, I don't know how much the Mother has told you?
Maria: Not much.
Captain: You're the ___10___ in a long line of governesses, who have come to look after my children since their mother died. I ___11___ that you will be an ___12___ on the last one. She stayed only ___13___.
Maria: What's wrong with the children, sir?
Captain: There was nothing wrong with the children, only the governesses. They were completely unable to ___14___. Without it, the house cannot be properly run. Please remember that, Fraulein.
Maria: Yes, sir.
Captain: Every morning you will ___15___ the children in their studies. I will not ___16___ them to dream away their summer holidays. Each afternoon they will march about the ground, breathing deeply. Bedtime is to be strictly observed. ___17___.
Maria: Excuse me, sir. When do they play?
Captain: You'll see to that they conduct themselves at all time with the utmost ___18___ and decorum, I'm placing you in command.
Maria: Yes, sir.

■ Song

beyond	on the brink	eager	time to think	canny
offer	older and wiser	unprepared	timid	beware
scared	what to do	a world of	take care of	fellows

Rolf (singing): You are sixteen, going on seventeen.
Baby, it's ___1___.
Better ___2___, be ___3___ and careful.
Baby, you're ___4___.
You are sixteen, going on seventeen.
___5___ will fall in line.
___6___ young lads and Ruez and Kaz will ___7___ you food and wine.
Totally ___8___ are you, to face ___9___ men.
___10___ and shy and ___11___ are you,
Things ___12___ your kin.
You need someone ___13___,
Telling you ___14___.
I am seventeen, going on eighteen.
I'll ___15___ you!

☞ 3. Story retelling

Direction: *Study the information in Reference 1 on the Dan Harmon story circle of this unit, and then retell the story of* The Sound of Music *by using specific details to support your ideas* (*Table 13.2*).

Table 13.2 Dan Harmon Story Circle of *The Sound of Music*

Dan Harmon Story Circle	The Sound of Music
You (Zone of comfort)	
Need (But they want something)	
Go (Enter an unfamiliar situation)	
Search (Adapt to it)	
Find (Get what they wanted)	
Take (Pay a heavy price for it)	
Return (Then return to their familiar situation)	
Change (Having changed)	

☞ 4. Sentence rearrangement

Direction: *Put the following sentences into the chronological order based on the story of* The Sound of music (*Table 13.3*).

Table 13.3 Sentences from *The Sound of Music*

Orders	Sentences
	I'm afraid you don't look much like a governess. Turn around, please.
	We should have put a cowbell around her neck.
	Fraulein Maria, I don't know how much the Mother has told you.
	How else could we get father's attention?
	I would have made myself a new dress but there wasn't time. I can make my own clothes.
	When you know the notes to sing, you can sing almost anything.
	These walls were not built to shut out problems.
	Once you have these notes in your heads, you can sing a million different tunes by mixing them up.
	What's wrong with the children, sir? There was nothing wrong with the children, only the governesses.

Section III English Chat Task

Direction: *Discuss the themes of this movie and organize your words on the specific themes (Table 13.4).*

Table 13.4 Themes of *The Sound of Music*

Themes	Questions about Themes	Answers (Key Words for Each Question)
Family	• What do you think a happy family is in the movie? • Why does the Trapp Family change governors frequently before Maria?	
Music	• How does the music influence the life of the Trapp family? • Which is your favourite song in the movie?	
Discipline	• What does the captain treat his children? • What does Maria think about the discipline of the captain?	

Themes	Questions about Themes	Answers (Key Words for Each Question)
Peace VS. War	• What kind of life does the captain pursue? • How does the captain behave facing the war?	
Patriotism and loyalty	• How do you evaluate Captain von Trapp? • How do you like Rolfe?	

Section IV EANLIC Party Tasks

☞ **1. Give a presentation on the theme of *The Sound of Music***

☞ **2. Role-play**

Direction: *Prepare this part in groups before class, and then do the role-play in class. Scan the QR code for role-play scripts.*

（1）The first time Maria meets the family of the von Trapp.
（2）When Maria teaches the children to sing.

☞ **3. Debate**

Direction: *Study the debate information in Reference 2 of this unit, and then deliver your debate by using debate techniques.*

（1）Should teachers love their students in the first place?
　　For: Teachers should love their students in the first place.
　　Against: Teachers don't have to love their students in the first place.
（2）Is it necessary to involve entertainments in education?
　　For: It is quite necessary to involve entertainments in education.
　　Against: It is unnecessary to involve entertainment in education.

Section V After-class Tasks

☞ **1. Mindmap drawing**

Direction: *Read Reference 1 of this unit once again, and then draw a mindmap of* The Sound of Music.

☞ **2. Movie review**

Direction: *Enjoy reading the movie review sample in Unit 12. Scan the QR code for the movie review sample and addresses attached for your further study.*

References

☞ 1. What is the Dan Harmon story circle?

This particular story structure is adapted from *The Hero's Journey*—which itself derives from the work of academic Joseph Campbell. The story circle lays out a kind of narrative arc that's commonly used in stories and emphasizes how almost all forms of storytelling have a cyclical nature. According to Harmon, the beauty of the story circle is that it can be applied to any type of story—and, conversely, be used to build any type of story, too.

It is a story structure divided into eight distinct parts following a protagonist's journey. These eight steps follow a character's pursuit of a goal outside of their normal world.

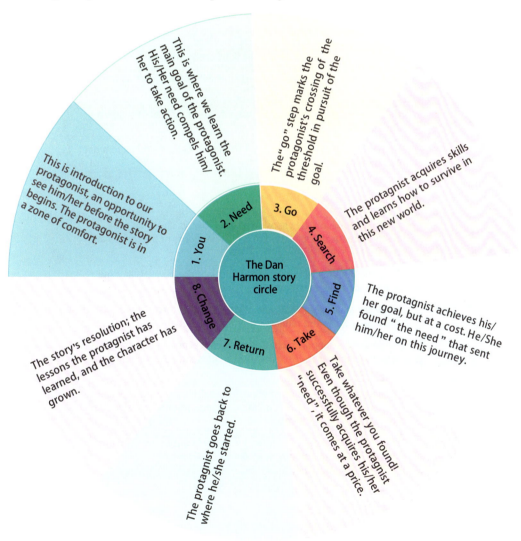

2. Debate techniques

We live in a world where we communicate with others all the time. Debate is a more formal way of communicating. It builds confidence and self-esteem in people. It is a valuable tool that helps us convey our ideas and thoughts coherently and passionately.

Debate techniques are essential tips that each of us must follow while writing a debate. These are used to persuade the audience why a specific argument or point of view is better than the other. The following are some practical techniques that you should keep in mind while organizing a debate.

Debate techniques

- **Benefits of debate techniques**
  - Help improve the critical thinking skills of the students.
  - Improve the listening and note-taking skills of students as they have to listen to the opponents closely.
  - Help the debaters learn better ways to state their points clearly and precisely.
  - Help the students structure their thoughts, beliefs, and experiences in a better way.

- **Techniques**
  - Form an opinion after choosing a topic. Always choose a topic with a practical application to which students or audience can relate.
  - Take enough time to research the topic and take notes. Take time to form a debate strategy.
  - Know the major arguments and try to memorize them. Make a list of the main points and rehearse them before debate.
  - Organize the support facts. Collect the facts and datas with credible sources for they are used to persuade the audience that your opinion is correct.
  - Connect to the audience emotionally. Real-life examples, personal experiences and a strong opening of your argument are good points to relate to the audience.
  - Find the right strategy to present. It requires public and debating speaking skills to present your points in debate.

Unit 14

The Shawshank Redemption

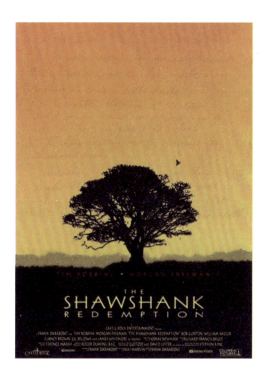

Unit Objectives:

1. Speaking skills:
   - Develop the ability to retell stories using the seven-point story structure effectively.
   - Learn to craft a convincing debate with given tips.
2. Emotional objectives:
   - Encourage students to cultivate a positive outlook, acknowledging the importance of having a positive mindset to overcome challenges.
   - Foster adaptability in adversity among students, equipping them with the skills and mindset needed to handle difficult situations.
   - Increase awareness of the power of hope and never giving up, helping students develop resilience and persistence in pursuit of their goals.

Section I Pre-class Tasks

The students are supposed to watch the movie of *The Shawshank Redemption* for at least 2 or 3 times ahead of the class, the first time for general understanding of the movie, and the second and third times for more detailed understanding and learning of English language, and then complete the following tasks before the class time.

☞ 1. Classic movie lines

Direction: *Read and recite the following lines from the movie.*

(1) Fear can hold you prisoner. Hope can set you free.

(2) Takes a strong man to save himself, and a great man to save another.

(3) Things that make you sad, one day, you will laugh out and say it.

☞ 2. Background knowledge

Direction: *Go through the passage and prepare to share the information in class.*

The film tells the story of Andy Dufresne, a banker who is sentenced to life in Shawshank State Penitentiary for the murder of his wife and her lover, despite his claims of innocence. During his time at the prison, he befriends a fellow inmate, who is capable of getting anything the prisoners could pay for. Andy buys a pick-axe and a poster of Rita Hayworth, and starts his plan of prison-break.

Andy first helps Captain Hadley with his tax and saves him a large sum of money, and then he helps more guards. Even Samuel Norton, the warden, uses him to do money laundering. Protected by the guards, he becomes a "respected" man in the prison which saves him from strenuous manual work and prevents him from being harassed by the prisoners.

A young prisoner, Tommy breaks up Andy's life in the prison. Tommy says he knows the real killer who kills Andy's wife. Any requests a retrial of this case, but is denied and punished. In order to keep Andy in the prison to help him with the money-laundering, the warden devises a plan to kill Tommy. Andy becomes very depressed and he breaks out of the prison.

It turns out that for 20 years, Andy has been digging a tunnel with the pick-axe and has covered the mouth with the poster of Rita Hayworth. After breaking out of the prison, he takes part of the black money in the warden's bank account and reveals the fact of the warden's embezzling money and accepting briberies. Red meets Andy again on a beach after being released on parole.

☞ 3. Vocabulary

Direction: *Learn these new words from this movie and try to use them at EANLIC night.*

redemption /rɪˈdempʃn/ *n.* the act of saving or state of being saved from the power of evil; the act of redeeming 拯救;救赎

confrontation /ˌkɒnfrʌnˈteɪʃn/ *n.* a situation in which there is an angry disagreement between people or groups who have different opinions 对抗,对峙,冲突

sneak /sniːk/ *v.* to go somewhere secretly, trying to avoid being seen 偷偷地走,溜

grant /ɡrɑːnt/ *v.* to agree to give sb. what they ask for, especially formal or legal permission to do sth. (尤指正式地或法律上)同意,准予,允许

testimony /ˈtestɪməni/ *n.* a formal written or spoken statement saying what you know to be true, usually in court 证词,证言,口供

sober /ˈsəʊbə(r)/ *v.* to make sb. behave or think in a more serious and sensible way; to become more serious and sensible 使变得沉重;使变得冷静

bullet /ˈbʊlɪt/ *n.* a small metal object that is fired from a gun 子弹,弹丸

coincidence /kəʊˈɪnsɪdəns/ *n.* the fact of two things happening at the same time by chance, in a surprising way (令人吃惊的)巧合,巧事

innocent /ˈɪnəsnt/ *adj.* not guilty of a crime, etc.; not having done sth. wrong 无辜的;清白的,无罪的

accuse /əˈkjuːz/ *v.* to say that sb. has done sth. wrong or is guilty of sth. 控告,控诉,谴责

footprint /ˈfʊtprɪnt/ *n.* a mark left on a surface by a person's foot or shoe or by an animal's foot 脚印;足迹

submit /səbˈmɪt/ *v.* to accept the authority, control or greater strength of sb./sth.; to agree to sth. because of this 顺从;屈服;投降;不得已接受

condone /kənˈdəʊn/ *v.* to accept behavior that is morally wrong or to treat it as if it were not serious 宽恕,饶恕,纵容

revenge /rɪˈvendʒ/ *n.* something that you do in order to make sb. suffer because they have made you suffer 报复,报仇

rehabilitate /ˌriːəˈbɪlɪteɪt/ *v.* to help sb. have a normal, useful life again after they have been very ill/sick or in prison for a long time 使(重病患者)康复,使(长期服刑者)恢复正常生活

reject /rɪˈdʒekt/ *v.* to refuse to accept or consider sth. 拒绝接受,不予考虑

cellblock /ˈselblɒk/ *n.* 囚犯室

warden /ˈwɔːdən/ *n.* a person who is responsible for taking care of a particular place and making sure that the rules are obeyed 管理人,看守人,监护人

acquaintance /əˈkweɪntəns/ *n.* a person that you know but who is not a close friend 认识的人,泛泛之交,熟人

infirmary /ɪnˈfɜːməri/ *n.* a special room in a school, prison, etc. for people who are ill/sick (学校、监狱等的)医务室

banker /ˈbæŋkə(r)/ *n.* a person who owns a bank or has an important job at a bank 银行老板(或要员),银行家

toothbrush /ˈtuːθbrʌʃ/ *n.* a small brush for cleaning your teeth 牙刷

quote /kwəʊt/ v. to tell a customer how much money you will charge them for a job, service or product 开价,出价,报价

tunnel /ˈtʌnl/ n. a long passage which has been made under the ground, usually through a hill or under the sea 隧道

inspection /ɪnˈspekʃn/ n. the act of looking closely at sth./sb., especially to check that everything is as it should be 检查,查看,审视

bruise /bruːz/ n. a blue, brown or purple mark that appears on the skin after sb. has fallen, been hit, etc. 青肿,淤伤,碰伤

privilege /ˈprɪvəlɪdʒ/ n. a special right or advantage that a particular person or group of people has 特殊利益,优惠待遇

budget /ˈbʌdʒɪt/ n. the money that is available to a person or an organization and a plan of how it will be spent over a period of time 预算

insane /ɪnˈseɪn/ adj. seriously mentally ill and unable to live in normal society 精神失常的,精神错乱的

contractor /ˈkɒntræktə/ n. a person or company that has a contract to do work or provide goods or services for another company 承包人,承包商,承包公司

cellmate /ˈselmeɪt/ n. a prisoner with whom another prisoner shares a cell 同牢难友

burglary /ˈbɜːɡləri/ n. the crime of entering a building illegally and stealing things from it 入室偷盗罪

launder /ˈlɔːndə(r)/ v. to move money that has been obtained illegally into foreign bank accounts or legal businesses so that it is difficult for people to know where the money came from 洗(钱)

trigger /ˈtrɪɡə(r)/ n. the part of a gun that you press in order to fire it (枪的)扳机

deposit /dɪˈpɒzɪt/ n. a sum of money that is given as the first part of a larger payment 订金

windowsill /ˈwɪndəʊsɪl/ n. a narrow shelf below a window, either inside or outside 窗沿,窗台

warrant /ˈwɒrənt/ n. a legal document that is signed by a judge and gives the police authority to do sth. 执行令,授权令

arrest /əˈrest/ v. if the police arrest sb., the person is taken to a police station and kept there because the police believe they may be guilty of a crime 逮捕,拘留

roadblock /ˈrəʊdblɒk/ n. a barrier put across the road by the police or army so that they can stop and search vehicles 路障

☞ 4. Character description

Direction: *Describe the main characters by using at least 5 adjectives in this movie with the reference of the words you have learned, and find examples in the movie to support your ideas (Table 14.1).*

Table 14.1 Main Characters in *The Shawshank Redemption*

Main Characters	Adjectives	Examples
Andy		
Red		
Brooks		
Hadley		
Norton		
Tommy		

Section II In-class Tasks

☞ 1. Workshop

Direction: *Discuss the questions with your classmates, and use the following sentence structures if it is possible.*

Sentence structures for citing evidence
- Based on what I watched in this movie …
- From what I watched in this movie, I understand that …
- Based on this movie, it can be concluded that … because …
- The most logical conclusion that can be drawn from this movie is that … because …
- … confirmed that …
- … explored the idea …

(1) What do you like or dislike about the *The Shawshank Redemption*?
(2) Is Andy innocent?
(3) How do you illustrate Red?
(4) How do you understand the word "institutionalization"?
(5) How do you like the ending of the movie?
(6) Who is your favourite character? Why?

☞ 2. Cloze

Direction: *Fill in the gaps in the following passages taken from the movie with the words or phrases given below.*

■ Passage 1

revenge	fingerprints	sinned	a death sentence	evidence
passion	bullets	likewise	accused	brutal
reload	condoned	footprints	victim	extra

Ladies and gentlemen, you've heard all the ___1___. You know all the facts. We have the ___2___ that the scene of the crime, we have ___3___, tire tracks, bullets on the ground bearing his ___4___. A broken bourbon bottle, ___5___ with fingerprints and most of all we have a beautiful young women and her lover lying dead in each other's arms. They had ___6___ but was their crime so great as to merit to ___7___? While you think about that … Think about this: A revolver holds six ___8___, not eight. I submit this was not a hot-blooded crime of ___9___ that at least could be understood, if not ___10___. No, this was ___11___ of a much more ___12___ cold-blooded nature. Consider this: four bullets per ___13___ no six shots fired, but eight, that means that he fired the gun empty and then stopped to ___14___. So that he could shoot each of them again, an ___15___ bullet per lover right in head.

■ **Passage 2**

beard	murderer	floats	closed book	tornado
Pacific Ocean	trigger	land on	expect	memory
complained	bad luck	Mexico	turn	the rest of my life

My wife used to say I'm a hard man to know, like a ___1___. ___2___ about it all the time. She was beautiful. God, I loved her. I didn't know how to show it: That's all. I killed her, Red. I didn't pull the ___3___ but I drove her away. That's why she died, because of me the way I am. That don't make you a ___4___. Bad husband, maybe. Feel bad about it if you want but you didn't pull the trigger. No, I didn't. Somebody else did. And I wound up in here. ___5___, I guess. It ___6___ around. It's got to ___7___ somebody. It was my ___8___. That's all. I was in the path of the ___9___. I just didn't ___10___ the storm would last as long as it has. Think you'll ever get out of here? Me? Yeah. One day, when I got a long, white ___11___ and two or three marbles left rolling around upstairs. They'll let me out. I tell you where I'd go. Zihuatanejo. Say what? Zihuatanejo. It's in ___12___. A little place on the ___13___. You know what the Mexicans say about the Pacific? They say it has no ___14___. That's where I want to live ___15___. A warm place with no memory. Open up a little hotel right on the beach. Buy some worthless old boat and fix it up new. Take my guests out charter fishing.

☞ **3. Story retelling**

Direction: *Study the information in Reference 1 on the seven-point story structure of this unit, and then retell the story of* The Shawshank Redemption *by using specific details to support your ideas (Table 14.2).*

Table 14.2　The Seven-point Story Structure of *The Shawshank Redemption*

The Seven-point Story Structure	The Shawshank Redemption
The hook	
Plot point 1	
Pinch point 1	
The midpoint	
Pinch point 2	
Plot point 2	
The resolution	

☞ 4. Sentence rearrangement

Direction: *Put the following sentences into the chronological order based on the story of* The Shawshank Redemption (*Table 14.3*).

Table 14.3　Sentences from *The Shawshank Redemption*

Orders	Sentences
	Along the way, I stopped and threw my gun into the Royal River. I feel I've been very clear on this point.
	My wife used to say I'm a hard man to know, like a closed book.
	Mr. Dufresne, describe the confrontation you had with your wife the night she was murdered.
	That's the way it is. It's down there and I'm in here. I guess it comes down to a simple choice. Get busy living or get busy dying.
	I have to remind myself that some birds aren't meant to be caged. Their feathers are just too bright.
	The police dragged that river for three days, and nary a gun was found.

continued

Orders	Sentences
	By the power vested in me by the state of Maine, I hereby order you to serve two life sentences back-to-back one for each of your victims. So be it!
	They say it has no memory. That's where I want to live the rest of my life.
	Bullets scattered on the ground bearing his fingerprints.
	In our hearts, there is a place that cannot be locked. That place is called hope.

Section III English Chat Task

Direction: *Discuss the themes of this movie and organize your words on the specific themes (Table 14.4).*

Table 14.4 Themes of *The Shawshank Redemption*

Themes	Questions about Themes	Answers (Key Words for Each Question)
Hope	• What is Red's attitude toward hope? • What is Andy's attitude toward hope?	
Institutionalization	• How do you illustrate Brooks? • What do you think of the management of *The Shawshank Redemption*?	
Redemption	• Who should be redeemed in *The Shawshank Redemption*? • How does Andy redeem Jimmy?	
Freedom VS Prison	• What does freedom mean to Andy? • What does prison mean to Red?	
Innocent VS Sinful	• Why does everybody in *The Shawshank Redemption* think they are innocent? • Why does Andy think he is sinful when he knows the truth of his wife's death?	

Section IV   EANLIC Party Tasks

☞ 1. Give a presentation on the theme of *The Shawshank Redemption*

☞ 2. Role-play

Direction: *Prepare this part in groups before class, and then do the role-play in class. Scan the QR code for role-play scripts.*
(1) The trial of Andy.
(2) When Andy has the last talk with Red in prison.

☞ 3. Debate

Direction: *Study the debate information in Reference 2 of this unit, and then craft a convincing debate with given tips.*
(1) Is institutionalization a good thing?
   For: Institutionalization is a very good thing.
   Against: Institutionalization is very harmful.
(2) Can people be truly free?
   For: People can be truly free.
   Against: People can never become truly free.

Section V   After-class Tasks

☞ 1. Mindmap drawing

Direction: *Read Reference 1 of this unit once again, and then draw a mindmap of* The Shawshank Redemption.

☞ 2. Movie review

Direction: *Enjoy reading the movie review sample in Unit 12. Scan the QR code for the movie review sample and addresses attached for your further study.*

References

☞ 1. The seven-point story structure

It's significant to map out your plots on organizing your story. That's why different writers have created story structures to help them write the best narratives.

The seven-point story structure is relatively new in the world of story structures. It was first popularized by sci-fi author and RPG-enthusiast Dan Wells at the 2013 Life, the Universe & Everything Conference. He took the structure outlined in the Star Trek Roleplaying Game Narrator's Guide and turned it into a system that he and many other authors claim to have used to build their story. Of course, these seven points aren't the only things happening in your story. But they are the key events that move your story from the beginning to the end. Let's look at them.

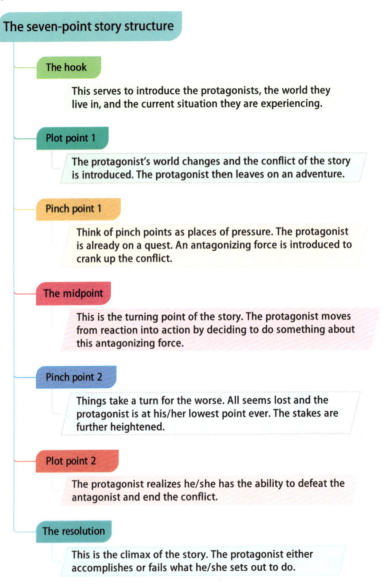

How to use the seven-point story structure in your story?

When planning a story with this structure, it's best to start at the resolution first, decide on the opposite of this ending, find the middle, and so on. So the plotting order would look more like this.

How to use it in your story?

Determine the resolution

Decide how you want the story to end. This gives you a sense of direction for where events should be heading. It helps you remember your hook is the opposite of your chosen ending.

Create your hook

Think about what your ending is and then create its opposite. So if the ending shows the characters as strong and confident, make them weak and cowardly in your hook.

Break the story into two with the midpoint

At this point, you have two events anchoring your story in place. The midpoint provides the event that turns the reaction into action.

- The first half is where the characters only react to everything around them.
- The second is where they proactively pursue their goals.

Flesh out the story using plot points 1 and 2

Plot point 1 is where your protagonists are pushed out of a familiar world and into a new one. This is usually where you introduce the main conflict.

Plot point 2 is different from plot point 1. It allows the characters to do the action on their own free will. This is your final step into the resolution.

Up the tension using pinch points 1 and 2

It's likely that the characters discovering something new or respond to a call of adventure. They are about to do something new, strange, or dangerous.

This is the time to introduce an element that raises the tension of the main conflict.

Plot point 1 reveals the main conflict.

Pinch point 2 ups the tension. But this time, the protagonists suddenly find themselves in a situation they have no control over or have no chance to win.

☞ 2. How to perform better in a debate?

People may come up with the most stunning content for their argument, but the fact is that in most cases, nearly one third of the marking criteria goes to your delivery of the material. While speaking passionately about poorly researched work probably won't win you a debate, marrying factual evidence with emotional conviction will. No matter how analytical and academic a debate is, your presentation will have a definite effect on your adjudicator, as well as your audience. In a tight match, your win may rest on the drama of your performance.

How to perform better in a debate?

Rhetoric

- Master the art of rhetoric to better your persuasion
- Assemble your argument with arrangement
  - Introduction. Express your message and why it's important to you and your audience.
  - Statement of fact. Break down the general thesis of your argument into smaller parts.
  - Confirmation. Craft your main argument, as well as reasons why your argument is a successful one.
  - Refutation. Acknowledge your opposition, giving some credence to their argument, before challenging their point-of-view.
  - Conclusion. Wrap up your main points of your argument and give instructions on what you want your audience to do or think.
- Express your argument as you improve your style
- Speak without paper by committing your speech to memory
- Amplify your performance techniques, highlighting your delivery

Delivery

- Eliminate filler words
- Find synonyms for overused language
- Speak slowly and clearly
- Deliver your rebuttals calmly

Behavior

- Consolidate your movement
  - Gestures can be helpful in elaborating on your points.
- Establish eye contact
  - Eye contact makes the crowd feel a trust in you in public-speaking setting.
- Diversify your tone
  - Change your tone throughout the debate will highlight the breadth of your argument.
- Master the dramatic pause
  - Dramatic and powerful pauses are the longest, but often the most successful.
- Close your debate with passion
  - Achieve this with a heightened tone of voice, or you can allow your speech to move a bit quicker than it normally would.

Unit 15 *Life Is Beautiful*

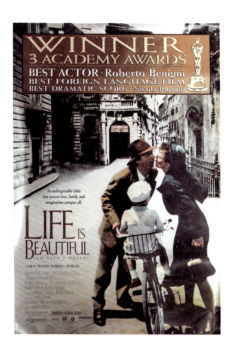

Unit Objectives:

1. Speaking skills:
   - Develop the ability to effectively retell the story shown in the movie using the Freytag's Pyramid structure.
   - Acquire the skills necessary to deliver a successful debate, including identifying winning keys and executing them effectively.

2. Emotional objectives:
   - Encourage students to deepen their appreciation of the importance of family values, emphasizing the significance of one's family as a source of support and strength.
   - Cultivate an attitude of gratitude amongst students towards their fathers and encourage them to cherish the love and support that their fathers provide.
   - Foster a sense of courage and bravery in students, instilling within them the confidence and drive to overcome adversity and pursue their goals with conviction.

Section I Pre-class Tasks

The students are supposed to watch the movie of *Life Is Beautiful* for at least 2 or 3 times ahead of the class, the first time for general understanding of the movie, and the second and third times for more detailed understanding and learning of English language, and then complete the following tasks before the class time.

☞ 1. Classic movie lines

Direction: *Read and recite the following lines from the movie.*

(1) Silence is the most powerful cry.
(2) This is a simple story, but not an easy one to tell. Like a fable, there is sorrow and like a fable, it is full of wonder and happiness.
(3) Nothing is more necessary than the unnecessary.

☞ 2. Background knowledge

Direction: *Go through the passage and prepare to share the information in class.*

Set in 1939 in Italy when Europe is shrouded in the dark cloud of WWII, the film tells a story of Guido, a seemingly clumsy, but kind and optimistic Jewish young man who is filled with beautiful longings for life. He goes to a small town and wants to open a bookstore with his friend. Mussolini implements racialism in Italy. Because Guido is Jewish, he is being discriminated. His application for opening a bookstore has been repeatedly denied. He has to work as a waiter in a hotel where he wins affection from the customers with his sincere service.

He meets Dora, a beautiful young lady and a teacher accidentally several times. He falls in love with her and tries very hard to win her love, but his efforts are futile. Hating her boyfriend, Rodolfo, Dora often hangs out with Guido. Guido helps Dora get away from being pestered by Rodolfo, which impresses her and she decides to marry him.

After their marriage, Guido gets to open his bookstore and they have a son, named Giosué. Their happy life comes to an end when the Nazi takes Guido and his son and is about to put them into the concentration camp. Though not a Jewish, Dora requests going to the concentration camp together with Guido and Giosué.

In the concentration camp, on the one hand, Guido seeks to contact Dora, telling her he and Giosué are safe; on the other hand, he racks his brains to figure out various ways to hide the truth of the concentration camp from Giosué. He convinces Giosué it is a game and the winner of the game will get a tank as a prize. Being curious and naive, Giosué takes what his father says to be true.

Upon liberation, the Nazi escape at a night. Hiding Giosué in a cupboard, Guido tries to rescue his wife in the women's prison, but he gets caught and killed. When he passes by the cupboard, Guido strides away optimistically and signals to Giosué not to come out. When the day breaks, Giosué crawls out of the cupboard. Standing in the yard, he sees a real tank rumbling up to him. An American soldier comes out and carries him to the tank.

3. Vocabulary

Direction: *Learn these new words from this movie and try to use them at EANLIC night.*

chaos /ˈkeɪɒs/　*n.* a state of complete confusion and lack of order 混乱, 杂乱, 紊乱

caress /kəˈres/　*v.* to touch sb./sth. gently, especially in a sexual way or in a way that shows affection 抚摩, 爱抚

brake /breɪk/　*n.* a device for slowing or stopping a vehicle 刹车, 制动器, 车闸

landlady /ˈlændleɪdi/　*n.* a woman from whom you rent a room, a house, etc. 女房东, 女地主

wasp /wɒsp/　*n.* a black and yellow flying insect that can sting 黄蜂, 胡蜂

sting /stɪŋ/　*v.* (of an insect or plant) to touch your skin or make a very small hole in it so that you feel a sharp pain 刺, 蜇, 叮

buggy /ˈbʌgi/　*n.* a light carriage for one or two people, pulled by one horse (由一匹马拉的单座或双座) 轻便马车

hiccup /ˈhɪkʌp/　*n.* a sharp, usually repeated, sound made in the throat, which is caused by a sudden movement of the diaphragm and that you cannot control 嗝, 呃逆

storehouse /ˈstɔːhaʊs/　*n.* a building where things are stored 仓库, 货栈

lobster /ˈlɒbstə(r)/　*n.* a sea creature with a hard shell, a long body divided into sections, eight legs and two large claws. Its shell is black but turns bright red when it is boiled 龙虾

willpower /ˈwɪlpaʊə/　*n.* the ability to control your thoughts and actions in order to achieve what you want to do 意志力

juggler /ˈdʒʌglə(r)/　*n.* someone who juggles in order to entertain people 抛接杂耍表演者

thigh /θaɪ/　*n.* the top part of the leg between the knee and the hip 大腿, 股

obscurity /əbˈskjʊərəti/　*n.* the state in which sb./sth. is not well-known or has been forgotten 默默无闻, 无名

riddle /ˈrɪdl/　*n.* a question that is difficult to understand, and that has a surprising answer, that you ask sb. as a game 谜, 谜语

dwarf /dwɔːf/　*n.* a creature like a small man, who has magic powers and who is usually described as living and working under the ground, especially working with metal (神话中有魔法的) 小矮人

lunatic /ˈluːnətɪk/　*n.* a person who does crazy things that are often dangerous 精神错乱者, 狂人

equation /ɪˈkweɪʒn/　*n.* a statement showing that two amounts or values are equal 方程, 方程式, 等式

leftover /ˈleftəʊvə(r)/　*n.* food that has not been eaten at the end of a meal 吃剩的食物, 残羹剩饭

nightstand /ˈnaɪtstænd/　*n.* a small table usually with shelves or drawers, that you have next to your bed（床边带抽屉的）小桌

fabulous /ˈfæbjələs/ *adj.* extremely good 极好的，绝妙的

reservation /ˌrezəˈveɪʃn/ *n.* an arrangement for a seat on a plane or train, a room in a hotel, etc. to be kept for you 预订，预约

lollipop /ˈlɒlipɒp/ *n.* a hard round or flat sweet/candy made of boiled sugar on a small stick 棒棒糖

referee /ˌrefəˈriː/ *n.* the official who controls the game in some sports（某些体育比赛的）裁判，裁判员

dues /djuːz/ *n.* charges, for example, to be a member of a club 应缴（如俱乐部会费）

trip /trɪp/ *v.* to catch your foot on sth. and fall or almost fall 绊，绊倒

hopscotch /ˈhɒpskɒtʃ/ *n.* a children's game played on a pattern of squares marked on the ground. Each child throws a stone into a square then hops (= jumps on one leg) and jumps along the empty squares to pick up the stone again 跳房子（儿童单足跳石子的游戏）

lightning /ˈlaɪtnɪŋ/ *n.* a flash, or several flashes, of very bright light in the sky caused by electricity 闪电

tease /tiːz/ *v.* to laugh at sb. and make jokes about them, either in a friendly way or in order to annoy or embarrass them 取笑，戏弄，揶揄，寻开心

cannon /ˈkænən/ *n.* an old type of large heavy gun, usually on wheels, which fires solid metal or stone balls（通常装有轮子并发射铁弹或石弹的旧式）大炮

gunfire /ˈɡʌnfaɪə(r)/ *n.* the repeated firing of guns; the sound of guns firing（接连不断的）炮火，炮火声

eliminate /ɪˈlɪmɪneɪt/ *v.* to kill sb., especially an enemy or opponent 消灭，干掉（尤指敌人或对手）

sacrifice /ˈsækrɪfaɪs/ *n.* the fact of giving up something important or valuable to you in order to get or do something that seems more important; something that you give up in this way 牺牲；舍弃

☞ 4. Character description

Direction：*Describe the main characters by using at least 5 adjectives in this movie with the reference of the words you have learned, and find examples in the movie to support your ideas (Table 15.1).*

Table 15.1　Main Characters in *Life Is Beautiful*

Main Characters	Adjectives	Examples
Guido		
Dora		
Joshua		
Guido's uncle		
Rodolfo（Dora's fiancé）		

Section II In-class Tasks

☞ 1. Workshop

Direction: *Discuss the questions with your classmatesm, and use the following sentence structures if it is possible.*

Sentence structures for presenting others' ideas

- However, ... stated that ...
- ... proposed that ...
- As identified by ..., ... demonstrated ...
- ... emphasizes the point that ...
- From ... perspective ...
- One argument in favor of ... is that ...

(1) What do you like or dislike about the movie?
(2) What do you think about the love between Guido and Dora?
(3) Do you know the background information when the movie was shot?
(4) How do you like Joshua?
(5) What is the main theme of the movie?

☞ 2. Cloze

Direction: *Fill in the gaps in the following passages taken from the movie with the words or phrases given below.*

Passage 1

| sick and tired of | tank | Spanish | kangaroo | hardware store | horses |
| How much | drugstore | | Chinese | From now on | probably |

Can we buy this for Mommy? ____1____ does it cost? Fifteen lire. It's ____2____ just a fake cake, like your ____3____. Let's go, Joshua. "No Jews or dogs ... allowed." Why aren't Jews or dogs allowed to go in? They just don't want Jews or dogs to go in. Everybody does what they want to. There's a ____4____ there. They don't let ____5____ people or ____6____ into his store. Further ahead, there's a ____7____. I was with a ____8____ friend of mine yesterday who had a ____9____. I said, "May we?" "No, we don't want any Chinese or kangaroos here." They don't like them. What can I tell you? We let everybody into our bookshop. No. ____10____, we'll write it too. Is there anybody you don't like? Spiders. What about you? I don't like Visigoths. Starting tomorrow we'll write ... "No spiders and Visigoths allowed." I'm ____11____ these Visigoths.

Passage 2

announce	mean	rules	hungry	thousand	on his back
starts	yell	prize	German	least	absolutely
sign	loudspeaker	snack	want to see	lose	jam sandwich

What did he say? He asked if anyone speaks ___1___. He's going to explain the camp's ___2___. Do you speak German? —No. The game ___3___ now. Whoever's here is here, whoever's not is not. The first one to get a ___4___ points wins. The ___5___ is a tank! Lucky him! Every day we'll ___6___ who's in the lead from that ___7___. The one with the ___8___ points has to wear a ___9___ saying "jackass"... right here ___10___. We play the part of the real ___11___ guys who ___12___. Whoever's scared loses points. You'll ___13___ your points for three things. One, if you cry. Two, if you ___14___ your mommy. Three, if you're ___15___ and you want a ___16___. Forget about it! It's easy to lose points for being hungry. Just yesterday I lost 40 points … because I ___17___ had to have a ___18___.

☞ **3. Story retelling**

Direction: *Study the information in Reference 1 on the Freytag's Pyramid of this unit, and then retell the story of* Life Is Beautiful *by using specific details to support your ideas* (Table 15.2).

Table 15.2　The Freytag's Pyramid of *Life Is Beautiful*

The Freytag's Pyramid	*Life Is Beautiful*
Introduction	
Rise, or rising action	
Climax	
Return, or fall	
Catastrophe	

☞ **4. Sentence rearrangement**

Direction: *Put the following sentences into the chronological order based on the story of* Life Is Beautiful (Table 15.3).

Table 15.3 Sentences from *Life Is Beautiful*

Orders	Sentences
	Joshua, make sure you treat the customers good! I'll be right back.
	You can lose all your points for any one of three things. One: If you cry. Two: If you want to see your mommy. Three: If you're hungry and you want a snack! Forget about it!
	We let everybody into our bookshop.
	The first one to get a thousand points wins. The prize is a tank! Lucky him!
	The one with the least points has to wear a sign saying "jackass"... right here on his back.
	They yell because everybody wants first prize.
	You have to get a thousand points. Whoever gets a thousand points wins a tank.
	What a place! Hurry up or they'll steal our places. We've got a reservation.
	He asked if anyone speaks German. He's going to explain the camp's rules.
	Starting tomorrow we'll write ... "No spiders and Visigoths allowed."

Section III English Chat Task

Direction: *Discuss the themes of this movie and organize your words on the specific themes (Table 15.4).*

Table 15.4 Themes of *Life Is Beautiful*

Themes	Questions about Themes	Answers (Key Words for Each Question)
Love	• Can you describe the love of Guido to Dora? • Can you describe the love of Guido to Joshua?	
Life	• How do you describe the life of Guido? • How do you describe the life of Dora?	
Imagination	• How does Guido explain the Nazi concentration camp to his son? • Does Joshua believe his father?	

continued

Themes	Questions about Themes	Answers (Key Words for Each Question)
Racial discrimination	• Why are Jews not allowed to enter some places? • Why doesn't Joshua know his grandma?	
War and cruelty	• Who are sent to the camp? • What does the shower really mean in the camp?	

Section IV   EANLIC Party Tasks

☞ **1. Give a presentation on the theme of** *Life Is Beautiful*

☞ **2. Role-play**

Direction: *Prepare this part in groups before class, and then do the role-play in class. Scan the QR code for role-play scripts.*

(1) No Jews or Dogs Allowed.

(2) When Guido is pretending to translate the German.

☞ **3. Debate**

Direction: *Study the debate information in Reference 2 of this unit, and then deliver a debate with provided winning keys.*

(1) Is Guido a great man or a liar?

　　For: Guido is a great man.

　　Against: Guido is a liar.

(2) Can people live well without telling lies?

　　For: People can live very well without telling lies.

　　Against: People can never live well without telling lies.

Section V   After-class Tasks

☞ **1. Mindmap drawing**

Direction: *Read Reference 1 of this unit once again, and then draw a mindmap of* Life Is Beautiful.

☞ **2. Movie review**

Direction: *Enjoy reading the movie review sample in Unit 12. Scan the QR* *code for the movie review sample and addresses attached for your further study.*

References

☞ 1. What is Freytag's Pyramid?

Like the hero's journey, the three-act structure, and newer models like Dan Harmon story circle, Freytag's Pyramid is simply one of many approaches that writers can use to create a complete and satisfying story for readers.

A note before we dive in: despite the fact that the pyramid was originally based on drama, Freytag's ideas are ultimately about storytelling, so they can also apply to both fiction and non-fiction writing-books, plays, TV, film, novels, memoirs, and short stories alike. You can learn more about it from the following mindmap.

Freytag's Pyramid structure

- **Introduction (Establish the characters and stakes)**
  - This beginning act is designed to orient the readers and set the story in motion. It asks and answers the question "Where am I?" followed by "What is happening?"

- **Rise, or rising action (Things seem to be on the up)**
  - The second act of Freytag's Pyramid is an in-between period of rising tension and escalating plot complexity.
  - The stakes, tension, and hope manifest as suspense, anxiety, or character development.

- **Climax (The world is turned upside-down)**
  - It's a turning point, and it changes everything. Sometimes, it takes the form of an inner realization, like a new awareness of one's cowardice and a resulting determination to face one's fears.
  - In tragedy, the climax is the point where the plot begins to unravel, with everything now taking a turn for the worse.

- **Return, or fall (Heading for tragedy)**
  - Once the protagonist crosses the point of no return, the plot speeds forward with a growing sense of inevitability.

- **Catastrophe (The inevitable becomes true)**
  - Catastrophe takes place when the character is finally brought to their lowest point. Like the climax, catastrophe may take many forms: a character could die, be financially ruined, or lose everyone's respect.
  - Whatever the catastrophe is, it's a forceful conclusion to the build-up of tension, the moment everything comes crashing down.

☞ 2. The keys to win a debate

To do well in a debate, you need to research and prepare. This means spending a lot of time writing and rewriting your speeches.

However, you can't just prewrite everything and expect to win. You also need to be able to think on your feet, write quickly, and respond promptly if you want to win.

To do this, you need to understand the key to victory.

The keys to win a debate

- **Listen to the opponent carefully**
  - Being a good listener is one of the most important debating skills.

- **Remain calm and reasonable at all times**
  - Remember that you are not to attack your opponent in a debate. Keep trying to convince them in friendly ways instead of losing your cool.
  - Shouting or insulting your debate partner helps him in the end. It makes you look unfriendly.

- **Use effective speech and grammar when speaking**
  - Focus on organizing your thoughts into complete, flowing sentences. Stay away from big or confusing words in an attempt to sound more intelligent.
  - Avoid words the audience may not understand and explain your points as needed.

- **Practise patience during the debate**
  - Debate in a respectful manner, and be willing to spend time explaining your position.
  - Don't expect to convince anyone right off the bat, for they may be very passionate about what they believe. So it requires patience to convience them.

- **Stay humble and prepared to lose a debate**
  - A skilled debater understands that sometimes the other person's arguments are stronger. If you find yourself unable to refute points, be honest and reasonable about it.
  - Take both wins and losses as an educational experience that makes you better equipped for the next debate.
  - Congratulate your opponent if you lose a debate. You might use it as an opportunity to figure out new ways to respond to criticisms of your beliefs.

Unit 16 Gone with the Wind

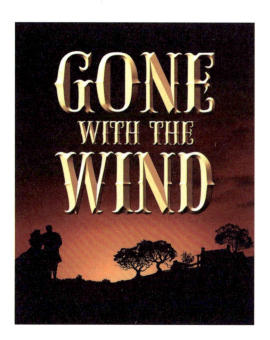

Unit Objectives:

1. Speaking skills:
   - Develop the ability to effectively retell the story shown in the movie using practical tips to enhance the delivery and impact of the retelling.
   - Acquire the skills and knowledge necessary to deliver an effective and persuasive debate, incorporating useful tips to improve the presentation.

2. Emotional objectives:
   - Cultivate a sense of courage amongst students, providing them with the tools and support necessary to survive and overcome adversity.
   - Foster students' awareness of the importance of being independent and self-reliant, emphasizing the benefits of personal responsibility and initiative.
   - Cultivate a love for a peaceful environment amongst students, highlighting the importance of peaceful coexistence and promoting the benefits of a harmonious and respectful community.

Section I Pre-class Tasks

The students are supposed to watch the movie of *Gone with the Wind* for at least 2 or 3 times ahead of the class, the first time for general understanding of the movie, and the second and third times for more detailed understanding and learning of English language, and then complete the following tasks before the class time.

☞ 1. Classic movie lines

Direction: *Read and recite the following lines from the movie.*

(1) Why, land is the only thing in the world worth working for … worth fighting for, worth dying for, because it's the only thing that lasts.

(2) With enough courage, you can do without a reputation.

(3) Most of the miseries of the world were caused by wars. And when the wars were over no one ever knew what they were about.

☞ 2. Background knowledge

Direction: *Go through the passage and prepare to share the information in class.*

The film is an epic and a romance. It tells the story of the tough life experience of a beautiful woman, Scarlett O'Hara in American south during the civil war period.

Before the start of the war life at the O'Hara plantation, Tara, the young Scarlett is in love with Ashley Wilkes. She is dismayed when she hears that he is to marry his cousin Melanie Hamilton and in a fit of anger, she decides to marry Melanie's brother, Charles, whom she doesn't love. Soon after Charles dies in the war and Scarlett is widowed. Now a widow, she still pines for the married Ashley and dreams of his return. Living in Atlanta, Scarlett sees the ravages that the war brings. She gets re-acquainted with Rhett Butler, whom she had first met at the Wilkes barbecue. With the war lost however, Rhett helps Scarlett return to Tara. She faces the hardship of keeping her family together and keeping Tara from being sold at auction to collect the taxes. She has become hardened and bitter and will do anything, including marrying her sister's beau, to ensure she will never again be poor and hungry. After becoming a widow for the second time, she finally marries Rhett but they soon find themselves working at cross-purposes, their relationship seemingly doomed from the outset.

☞ 3. Vocabulary

Direction: *Learn these new words and expression(s) from this movie and try to use them at EANLIC night.*

expel /ɪkˈspel/ *v.* to officially make sb. leave a school or an organization 把……开除(或除名)

spoil /spɔɪl/ *v.* to change sth. good into sth. bad, unpleasant, useless, etc. 破坏, 搞坏, 糟蹋, 毁掉

slam /slæm/ *v.* to shut, or to make sth. shut, with a lot of force, making a loud noise (使……)砰地关上

plow /plaʊ/ *v.* to dig and turn over a field or other area of land with a plough 犁(田), 耕(地), 翻(土)

dismiss /dɪsˈmɪs/ *v.* to officially remove sb. from their job 解雇, 免职, 开除

overseer /ˈəʊvəsɪə(r)/ *n.* a person whose job is to make sure that other workers do their work 监工, 工头

appetite /ˈæpɪtaɪt/ *n.* physical desire for food 食欲, 胃口

silly /ˈsɪli/ *adj.* showing a lack of thought, understanding or judgement 愚蠢的, 不明事理的, 没头脑的, 傻的

flatter /ˈflætə(r)/ *v.* to say nice things about sb., often in a way that is not sincere, because you want them to do sth. for you or you want to please them 奉承, 讨好, 向……谄媚

accuse /əˈkjuːz/ *v.* to say that sb. has done sth. wrong or is guilty of sth. 控告, 控诉, 谴责

insincere /ˌɪnsɪnˈsɪə(r)/ *adj.* saying or doing sth. that you do not really mean or believe 不诚恳的, 不真心的

fickle /ˈfɪkl/ *adj.* often changing their mind in an unreasonable way so that you cannot rely on them 反复无常的

reputation /ˌrepjuˈteɪʃn/ *n.* the opinion that people have about what sb./sth. is like, based on what has happened in the past 名誉, 名声

approval /əˈpruːvl/ *n.* the feeling that sb./sth. is good or acceptable; a positive opinion of sb./sth. 赞成; 同意

assert /əˈsɜːt/ *v.* to make other people recognize your right or authority to do sth., by behaving firmly and confidently 维护自己的权利(或权威)

insult /ɪnˈsʌlt/ *v.* to say or do sth. that offends sb. 辱骂, 侮辱, 冒犯

misery /ˈmɪzəri/ *n.* something that causes great suffering of mind or body 不幸的事, 痛苦的事

equip /ɪˈkwɪp/ *v.* to provide sb./sth. with the things that are needed for a particular purpose or activity 配备, 装备

arrogance /ˈærəɡəns/ *n.* the behaviour of a person when they feel that they are more important than other people, so that they are rude to them or do not consider them 傲慢, 自大

offend /əˈfend/ *v.* to make sb. feel upset because of sth. you say or do that is rude or embarrassing 得罪, 冒犯

passion /ˈpæʃn/ *n.* a very strong feeling of love, hatred, anger, enthusiasm, etc. 强烈情感; 激情

flock /flɒk/ *v.* to go or gather together somewhere in large numbers 群集, 聚集, 蜂拥

Expression(s)

trifle with sb.   to treat sb./sth. without genuine respect（尤用于否定句）怠慢，小看

figure out   find the solution to (a problem or question) or understand the meaning of 想出，理解，弄清

☞ 4. Character description

Direction：Describe the main characters by using at least 5 adjectives in this movie with the reference of the words you have learned, and find examples in the movie to support your ideas (Table 16.1).

Table 16.1   Main Characters in *Gone with the Wind*

Main Characters	Adjectives	Examples
Scarlett		
Rhett Butler		
Ashley		
Melanie Hamilton		
Gerald O'Hara		
Ellen		
Mammy		
Belle Watling		

Section II   In-class Tasks

☞ 1. Workshop

Direction：Discuss the questions with your classmates, and use the following sentence structures if it is possible.

Sentence structures for showing the outcome
- These factors contribute to …
- The outcome is …
- There is growing support for the point that …
- Considering … it can be concluded that …
- This topic has fostered a debate on …
- The result gathered in the study strongly suggests that …

(1) Discuss the importance of Tara to Scarlett.
(2) What is the relationship between Mammy and the rest of the members in the family?
(3) What is Ashley's attitude towards the war?
(4) What are the differences between the South and the North in terms of economy?
(5) Who would win the war, according to Butler, the South or the North? And why?
(6) Why does Scarlett decide to marry Melanie's brother?
(7) For what, does Scarlett marry her sister's beau?
(8) How does Bonnie die?
(9) How does the war affect Scarlett?
(10) Who is your favourite character in this movie? Why?

☞ 2. Cloze

Direction: *Fill in the gaps in the following dialogues taken from the movie with the words or phrases given below.*

■ Dialogue 1

gentlemen	apologies	insulted	treacherous	winning a war with words
fleet	arrogance	equipped	hinting	what they were about
difference	spoiling	plainly	starve us to death	look over your place
offends	union	decent	dreams of victory	were caused by wars

Gerald O'Hara: (The men are discussing the prospect of going to war with the North) And what does the captain of our troops say?

Ashley: Well, gentlemen, if Georgia fights, I go with her. But like my father I hope that the Yankees let us leave the ___1___ in peace.

Man: But Ashley, Ashley, they've ___2___ us!

Charles Hamilton—Her Brother: You can't mean you don't want war!

Ashley: Most of the miseries of the world ___3___. And when the wars were over, no one ever knew ___4___.

Gerald O'Hara: (The other men protest) Now, gentlemen, Mr. Butler has been up North I hear. Don't you agree with us, Mr. Butler?

Rhett Butler: I think it's hard ___5___, gentlemen.

Charles Hamilton—Her Brother: What do you mean, sir?

Rhett Butler: I mean, Mr. Hamilton, there's not a cannon factory in the whole South.

Man: What ___6___ does that make, sir, to a gentleman?

Rhett Butler: I'm afraid it's going to make a great deal of difference to a great many ___7___, sir.

Charles Hamilton—Her Brother: Are you ___8___, Mr. Butler, that the Yankees can lick us?

Rhett Butler: No, I'm not hinting. I'm saying very ___9___ that the Yankees are better ___10___ than we. They've got factories, shipyards, coalmines … and a ___11___ to bottle up our harbors and ___12___. All we've got is cotton, and slaves and … ___13___.

Man: That's ___14___!

Charles Hamilton—Her Brother: I refuse to listen to any renegade talk!

Rhett Butler: Well, I'm sorry if the truth ___15___ you.

Charles Hamilton—Her Brother: ___16___ aren't enough, sir. I hear you were turned out of West Point, Mr. Rhett Butler. And that you aren't received in a ___17___ family in Charleston. Not even your own.

Rhett Butler: I apologize again for all my shortcomings. Mr. Wilkes, Perhaps you won't mind if I walk about and ___18___. I seem to be ___19___ everybody's brandy and cigars and … ___20___.

- **Dialogue 2**

soldier	silly	leave me	memory	I've ever loved any woman	in the eyes
bullet	hold	loving me	selfish	understand or forgive myself	being an idiot
alone	alike	pieces	battle	sending a soldier to his death	shrewd
I love you		longer		to forgive me	arms

Scarlett: (pleads with Rhett as he is about to leave to join the Confederate Army) Oh, Rhett! Please, don't go! You can't ___1___! Please! I'll never forgive you!

Rhett Butler: I'm not asking you ___2___. I'll never ___3___. And if a ___4___ gets me, so help me, I'll laugh at myself for ___5___. There's one thing I do know … and that is that ___6___, Scarlett. In spite of you and me and the whole ___7___ world going to ___8___ around us, I love you. Because we're ___9___. Bad lots, both of us. ___10___ and ___11___. But able to look things ___12___ as we call them by their right names.

Scarlett: (struggles) Don't ___13___ me like that!

Rhett Butler: (holds her tighter) Scarlett! Look at me! I've loved you more than ___14___ and I've waited for you ___15___ than I've ever waited for any woman. (kisses her forehead)

Scarlett: (turns her face away) Let me ___16___!

Rhett Butler: (forces her to look him in the eyes) Here's a ___17___ of the South who loves you, Scarlett. Wants to feel your ___18___ around him, wants to carry the ___19___ of your kisses into ___20___ with him. Never mind about ___21___, you're a woman ___22___ with a beautiful memory. Scarlett! Kiss me!

☞ 3. Story retelling

Direction: *Study the information in Reference 1 on "how to tell a story effectively" of this unit, and then retell the story of* Gone with the Wind *by using specific details to support your ideas (Table 16.2).*

Table 16.2 How to Tell a Story Effectively

How to Tell a Story Effectively	Your Notes
Choose a clear central message	
Embrace conflict	
Have a clear structure	
Mine your personal experiences	
Engage your audience	
Observe good storytellers	
Narrow the scope of your story	

☞ 4. Sentence rearrangement

Direction: *Put the following sentences into the chronological order based on the story of* Gone with the Wind *(Table 16.3).*

Table 16.3 Sentences from *Gone with the Wind*

Orders	Sentences
	It seems we've been at cross purposes, doesn't it? But it's no use now. As long as there was Bonnie, there was a chance that we might be happy.
	I liked to think that Bonnie was you, a little girl again, before the war, and poverty had done things to you. She was so like you, and I could pet her, and spoil her, as I wanted to spoil you.

continued

Orders	Sentences
	I'm going back to Charleston, back where I belong.
	I'm leaving you, my dear. All you need now is a divorce and your dreams of Ashley can come true.
	Please don't go on with this. Leave us some dignity to remember out of our marriage. Spare us this last.
	I'm through with everything here. I want peace. I want to see if somewhere there isn't something left in life of charm and grace.
	What gentlemen says and what they thinks is two different things.
	Oh Rhett, do listen to me, I must have loved you for years, only I was such a stupid fool, I didn't know it. Please believe me, you must care!
	You think that by saying, "I'm sorry," all the past can be corrected. Here, take my handkerchief. Never, at any crisis of your life, have I known you to have a handkerchief.
	I'm going to have a good time today, and do my eating at the barbeque.

Section III   English Chat Task

Direction: *Discuss the themes of this movie and organize your words on the specific themes (Table 16.4).*

Table 16.4   Themes of *Gone with the Wind*

Themes	Questions about Themes	Answers (Key Words for Each Question)
Positive attitude during social transformation	• What's your view on Scarlet's obsession with Ashley? • How do you understand Scarlet's saying "I'll think it tomorrow, after all tomorrow is another day"?	
Survival	• Why does Scarlet marry Frank Kennedy? • What's Scarlet's real purpose of going to visit Rhett in jail?	

Section IV EANLIC Party Tasks

☞ 1. Give a presentation on the theme of *Gone with the Wind*

☞ 2. Role-play

Direction: *Prepare this part in groups before class, and then do the role-play in class. Scan the QR code for role-play scripts.*

(1) Rhett Butler is leaving Scarlett.
(2) Mammy is trying to talk Scarlett into eating before going to the Wilkes'.

☞ 3. Debate

Direction: *Study the debate information in Reference 2 of this unit, and then deliver an effective and persuasive debate.*

(1) Does marrying men Scarlet doesn't love show that she is a responsible women?
   For: Marrying men she doesn't love shows that Scarlet is an irresponsible woman.
   Against: Marrying men she doesn't love shows that Scarlet is a responsible woman.
(2) Does war help people to build better lives?
   For: War helps people to build better lives.
   Against: War destroys people's lives.

Section V After-class Tasks

☞ 1. Mindmap drawing

Direction: *Read Reference 1 of this unit once again, and then draw a mindmap of* Gone with the Wind.

☞ 2. Movie review

Direction: *Enjoy reading the movie review sample of* Gone with the Wind. *Scan the QR code for the movie review sample and addresses attached for your further study.*

References

☞ 1. How to tell a story effectively?

Storytelling is a powerful tool that great leaders use to motivate the masses and masterful writers harness to create classic literature. If you're just getting started writing and telling stories, here are some storytelling tips that can help you strengthen your narratives and engage your audience.

How to tell a story effectively?

- **Choose a clear central message**
  - A great story usually progresses towards a central moral or message. So, it's important to be very clear on the central theme or point that you are building your story around.

- **Embrace conflict**
  - Storytellers craft narratives that have all sorts of obstacles and hardships strewn in the path of their protagonists. In order to have a happy ending, audience have to watch the main characters struggle to achieve their goals.

- **Have a clear structure**
  - A story must have a beginning, a middle, and an end. A successful story starts with an inciting incident, leads into rising action, builds to a climax and finally settles into a satisfying resolution.

- **Mine your personal experiences**
  - Think about important experiences in your real life and how you might be able to craft them into narratives.

- **Engage your audience**
  - Great storytelling requires you to connect with your audience. It helps you captivate them.

- **Observe good storytellers**
  - Learn how to craft and deliver a narrative by watching storytellers you admire relate their own stories.
  - Look for good storytellers and learn through observation: "How do they craft a successful story?"

- **Narrow the scope of your story**
  - Do not include every detail in your story, choose the main points. Do not overwhelm your audience with unnecessary backstory or plot points.
  - Choose a clear beginning and end for your story, and then write the key plot events as bullet points between them.

☞ 2. Debating skills

Debating is a skill that can be useful in many different situations, from winning arguments in daily life to making a case in a professional setting. A good debater is able to think on his feet, anticipate his opponent's arguments and present a clear and convincing argument of his own. We will learn the detailed debating skills in the following mindmap.

Debating skills

Critical thinking
- It allows you to evaluate arguments and make decisions based on logic and evidence.

Public speaking
- Public speaking skills are important for debaters because they allow them to deliver their arguments in the most effective way possible.

Persuasive writing
- It is an important skill for debaters because it allows them to convince their opponents' point of view.

Argumentation
- It is the process of making an argument. In argumentation, you will make a claim, provide evidence to support that claim, and then defend your claim against objections.

Research
- It allows you to support your arguments with facts and figures.
- It makes your argument more persuasive and helps you win over your audience.
- It also helps you identify weaknesses in your opponent's arguments.

Analysis
- It is the process of breaking down a topic or issue into smaller parts in order to understand it better.
- It helps you make better decisions and arguments.
- It can help you find supporting evidence for your argument.

Teamwork
- It allows debaters to work together to formulate arguments, research topics and prepare for debates.
- It requires good communication, collaboration and compromise. Debaters who are able to work well together are more likely to be successful in a debate.

Time management
- It allows debaters to plan and execute their arguments efficiently. Good time management means being able to prioritize tasks, set deadlines and stick to them.

Creativity
- It allows debaters to come up with new arguments and rebuttals on the fly.
- It allows debaters to think outside the box and come up with unique ways to frame arguments.

Unit 17

Pride and Prejudice (2005)

Unit Objectives:

1. Speaking skills:
   - Develop the ability to retell the story in this movie using the given format, thereby improving storytelling proficiency.
   - Acquire the skills and knowledge necessary to deliver persuasive and effective debate speeches, thus honing and enhancing one's debating abilities.

2. Emotional objectives:
   - Cultivate students' awareness of the dangers of pride and prejudice, emphasizing the problems that can arise from negative attitudes and beliefs.
   - Teach students to never judge a book by its cover, encouraging them to look beyond appearances and to examine people and situations in a more nuanced and thoughtful way.
   - Foster a healthy and positive attitude towards marriage, highlighting the importance of mutual respect, understanding, and support in building successful and fulfilling partnerships.

Section I Pre-class Tasks

The students are supposed to watch the movie of *Pride and Prejudice* (2005) for at least 2 or 3 times ahead of the class, the first time for general understanding of the movie, and the second and third times for more detailed understanding and learning of English language, and then complete the following tasks before the class time.

☞ 1. Classical movie lines

Direction: *Read and recite the following lines from the movie.*

(1) I'm willing to put them aside and ask you to end my agony.

(2) It is a truth universally acknowledged that a single man in possession of a good fortune must be in want of a wife.

(3) It is very often nothing but our own vanity that deceives us.

☞ 2. Background knowledge

Direction: *Go through the passage and prepare to share the information in class.*

The story tells a humorous story of love and life of the English during the Georgian era. Mr. Bennet is an English gentleman. He and his wife live in Hartfordshire with their daughters: Jane, Elizabeth, Mary, Kitty and Lydia. The five daughters vary greatly from each other in their personality. Jane is beautiful; Elizabeth is clever; Mary is bookish; Kitty is immature and Lydia is wild. The Bennets face an issue concerning the inheritance of the family property. If Mr. Bennet dies, their house will be inherited by a distant cousin who they have never met. So it's very important for the Bennets daughters to marry good husbands. The happiness and security of the family hang on the daughters' good marriage.

With the arrival of a rich gentleman, Mr. Bingley, the uneventful life of the Bennets comes to an end. Mr. Bingley rents a large house for spending the summer there. Coming with Mr. Bingley are his sister, Caroline and his friend, the rich but proud Mr. Darcy. After the meeting at the ball, love grows in Mr. Bingley and Jane while Elizabeth and Mr. Darcy jump to a hasty prejudgment on each other. The Bennet sisters go through many trials and tribulation (concerning class, gossip and scandal) until they finally find their own love and happiness.

☞ 3. Vocabulary

Direction: *Learn these new words and expression(s) from this movie and try to use them at EANLIC night.*

tease /tiːz/ *v.* to laugh at sb. and make jokes about them, either in a friendly way or in order to annoy or embarrass them 取笑,戏弄,揶揄,寻开心

compassion /kəmˈpæʃn/ *n.* a strong feeling of sympathy for people who are suffering and a desire to help them 同情，怜悯

nerves /nɜːvz/ *n.* any of the long thin fibres that transmit messages between your brain and other parts of your body 神经

companion /kəmˈpæniən/ *n.* a person or an animal that travels with you or spends a lot of time with you 旅伴，伴侣，陪伴

amiable /ˈeɪmiəbl/ *adj.* pleasant; friendly and easy to like 和蔼可亲的，亲切友好的

hearty /ˈhɑːti/ *adj.* showing that you feel strongly about sth. 强烈的，尽情的

consent /kənˈsent/ *n.* permission to do sth., especially given by sb. in authority 同意，准许，允许

slippers /ˈslɪpəz/ *n.* loose, soft shoes that you wear at home 拖鞋

re-trim /ˌriːˈtrɪm/ *v.* to trim again 重新修剪

bonnet /ˈbɒnɪt/ *n.* a hat tied with strings under the chin, worn by babies and, especially in the past, by women（带子系于下巴的）童帽，旧式女帽

agreeable /əˈɡriːəbl/ *adj.* pleasant and easy to like 愉悦的，讨人喜欢的，宜人的

splendid /ˈsplendɪd/ *adj.* excellent; very good (old-fashioned) 极佳的；非常好的

dine /daɪn/ *v.* (formal) to eat dinner 进餐，用饭

sore /sɔː(r)/ *adj.* if a part of your body is sore, it is painful, and often red, especially because of infection or because a muscle has been used too much（发炎）疼痛的，酸痛的

redecorate /ˌriːˈdekəreɪt/ *v.* to put new paint and/or paper on the walls of a room or house（用涂料或壁纸）重新装饰，再次装修

diligently /ˈdɪlɪdʒəntli/ *adv.* with diligence 勤勉地，勤奋地

incapable /ɪnˈkeɪpəbl/ *adj.* not able to do sth. 没有能力做某事

deceive /dɪˈsiːv/ *v.* to make sb. believe sth. that is not true 欺骗，蒙骗，诓骗

affectionate /əˈfekʃənət/ *adj.* showing caring feelings and love for sb. 表示关爱的

burden /ˈbɜːdn/ *n.* a duty, responsibility, etc. that causes worry, difficulty or hard work（义务、责任等的）重担，负担

flatter /ˈflætə(r)/ *v.* to choose to believe sth. good about yourself and your abilities, especially when other people do not share this opinion 自命不凡

mistress /ˈmɪstrəs/ *n.* (in the past) the female head of a house, especially one who employed servants（尤指旧时雇用仆人的）女主人，主妇

impudence /ˈɪmpjədəns/ *n.* the trait of being rude and impertinent 鲁莽，无礼，无礼的言行

overbearing /ˌəʊvəˈbeərɪŋ/ *adj.* trying to control other people in an unpleasant way 专横的，飞扬跋扈的

seizure /ˈsiːʒə(r)/ *n.* a sudden attack of an illness, especially one that affects the brain（疾病，尤指脑病的）侵袭，发作

transfer /trænsˈfɜː(r)/ *v.* to move from one job, school, situation, etc. to another; to arrange for sb. to move（使）调动；转职；转学；改变（环境）

oblige /əˈblaɪdʒ/ *v.* to help sb. by doing what they ask or what you know they want（根据要

求或需要)帮忙,效劳

covey /ˈkʌvi/ *n.* a small flock of grouse or partridge (松鸡或山鹑的)一小群,一小窝

untoward /ˌʌntəˈwɔːd/ *adj.* unusual and unexpected, and usually unpleasant 异常的;意外的;不幸的;棘手的

Expression(s)

tend to *v.* to care for sb./sth. 照料,照管,护理

4. Character description

Direction: *Describe the main characters by using at least 5 adjectives in this movie with the reference of the words you have learned, and find examples in the movie to support your ideas (Table 17.1).*

Table 17.1 Main Characters in *Pride and Prejudice* (2005)

Main Characters	Adjectives	Examples
Mr. Bennet		
Mrs. Bennet		
Jane Bennet		
Elizabeth Bennet		
Mary Bennet		
Kitty Bennet		
Lydia Bennet		
Mr. Darcy		
Mr. Bingley		
Caroline Bingley		
Mr. Collins		

Section II In-class Tasks

1. Workshop

Direction: *Discuss the questions with your classmates, and use the following sentence structures if it is possible.*

Sentence structures for helping understanding

- I don't understand what you mean by …
- Could you give an example of what you mean by …?

- I'm not sure I understand your question; could you rephrase it?
- Could you explain ... further?
- When you say ... it seems like you are implying ... Is that what you mean?

(1) Among the five daughters, whom does Mr. Bennet love most? Why?

(2) What's Elizabeth's first impression of Mr. Darcy?

(3) Why do Darcy and Bingley's sisters meddle in Bingley and Jane's romance?

(4) Why does Lady Catherine try to stop Darcy and Elizabeth's marriage?

(5) Who is Wickham? Would you please share some information about him?

(6) How does Lydia's elopement affect the Bennets?

(7) Who is your favourite character in this movie? Why?

☞ 2. Cloze

Direction: *Fill in the gaps in the following dialogues taken from the movie with the words or phrases given below.*

■ **Dialogue 1**

making amends	feelings	scarcely allowed myself	affections and wishes
body and soul	suspect	trifle with	bewitched	it was all for you
amends	be parted from		what they were	silence

Elizabeth: I couldn't sleep.

Darcy: Nor I. My aunt …

Elizabeth: Yes. She was here.

Darcy: How can I ever make ___1___ for such behaviour?

Elizabeth: After what you have done for Lydia, and I ___2___ for Jane also, it is I who should be ___3___.

Darcy: You must know. Surely you must know ___4___. You are too generous to ___5___ me. I believe you spoke with my aunt last night and it has taught me to hope as I had ___6___ before. If your feelings are still ___7___ last April, tell me so at once. My ___8___ have not changed, but one word from you will ___9___ me forever. If, however, your ___10___ have changed, I would have to tell you, you have ___11___ me, ___12___, and I love … I love … I love you. I never wish to ___13___ you from this day on.

■ **Dialogue 2**

union	inferior	once and for all	insulted	impossible
scandalously	elopement	offer	reason	engagement
infancy	expense	further	engaged to	polluted

Lady Catherine: Has my nephew made you an ___1___ of marriage?

Elizabeth: Your Ladyship has declared it to be ___2___.

Lady Catherine: Let me be understood. Mr. Darcy is ___3___ my daughter. Now, what have you to say?

Elizabeth: Only this. If that is the case, you can have no ___4___ to suppose he would make an offer to me.

Lady Catherine: You selfish girl! This ___5___ has been planned since their ___6___. Do you think it can be prevented by a young woman of ___7___ birth whose own sister's ___8___ resulted in a ___9___ patched-up marriage only achieved at the ___10___ of your uncle? Heaven and Earth, are the shades of Pemberley to be thus ___11___? Now tell me ___12___, are you engaged to him?

Elizabeth: I am not.

Lady Catherine: And will you promise never to enter into such an ___13___?

Elizabeth: I will not, and I certainly never shall. You have ___14___ me in every possible way and can now have nothing ___15___ to say. I must ask you to leave immediately.

☞ 3. Story retelling

Direction: *Study the information on ways to practise retelling stories in Reference 1 of this unit, and then retell the story of* Pride and Prejudice *by using specific details to support your ideas (Table 17.2).*

Table 17.2　Ways to Practise Retelling Stories

Practise Retelling Stories	Your Notes
Give students a purpose for retelling	
Provide a predictable structure to set students up for success	
Identify the theme	
Respect students' individual preferences in ways of practising retelling	

☞ 4. Sentence rearrangement

Direction: *Put the following sentences into the chronological order based on the story of* Pride and Prejudice *(2005) (Table 17.3).*

Table 17.3 Sentences from *Pride and Prejudice* (2005)

Orders	Sentences
	Not all of us can afford to be romantic, Lizzy.
	I cannot believe that anyone can deserve you ... but it appears I am overruled. So, I heartily give my consent.
	Now if every man in the room does not end the evening in love with you then I am no judge of beauty.
	Men are either eaten up with arrogance or stupidity. If they are amiable, they are so easily led they have no minds of their own whatsoever.
	What are men compared to rocks and mountains?
	Sir, I am honored by your proposal, but I regret that I must decline it.
	When you have five daughters, Lizzie, tell me what else will occupy your thoughts, and then perhaps you will understand.
	If any young men come for Mary or Kitty, for heaven's sake, send them in. I'm quite at my leisure.
	Miss Elizabeth, I have struggled in vain and I can bear it no longer. These past months have been a torment.
	Men are either eaten up with arrogance or stupidity. If they are amiable, they are so easily led they have no minds of their own whatsoever.

Section III English Chat Task

Direction: *Discuss the themes of this movie and organize your words on the specific themes (Table 17.4).*

Table 17.4 Themes of *Pride and Prejudice* (2005)

Themes	Questions about Themes	Answers (Key Words for Each Question)
The danger of pride and prejudice	• What causes the obstacle in the path of Elizabeth and Darcy's romance? • What causes Elizabeth's "prejudice" against Mr. Darcy?	
Love and marriage	• Why does Mr. Darcy interfere with Jane and Bingley's romance? • Why does Mr. Darcy say that he has fought against his better judgment, his family's expectation, the inferiority of Elizabeth's birth, his rank and circumstance to love her?	

continued

Themes	Questions about Themes	Answers (Key Words for Each Question)
Love and social status	• How social status causes the obstacle in Darcy and Elizabeth's romance? • How does Elizabeth view love and social status?	
Family relationship	• What's the difference between Jane and Elizabeth? • Does the difference affect the relationship between Jane and Elizabeth? Why?	

Section IV   EANLIC Party Tasks

☞ **1. Give a presentation on the theme of *Pride and Prejudice* (2005)**

☞ **2. Role-play**

Direction: *Prepare this part in groups before class, and then do the role-play in class. Scan the QR code for role-play scripts.*

(1) Elizabeth rejects Mr. Darcy's proposal.

(2) Elizabeth and Mr. Darcy are arguing about the reason why Mr. Darcy's proposal gets rejected.

☞ **3. Debate**

Direction: *Study the debate information in Reference 2 of this unit, and then deliver a debate with debate skills.*

(1) Should love or social status be considered the most important factor in marriage?

   For: Love should be the most important consideration in marriage.

   Against: Social status should be the most important consideration in marriage.

(2) Is the relationship between Elizabeth and Mr. Darcy healthy?

   For: The relationship between Elizabeth and Mr. Darcy is quiet healthy.

   Against: The relationship between Elizabeth and Mr. Darcy is problematic.

Section V   After-class Tasks

☞ **1. Mindmap drawing**

Direction: *Read Reference 1 of this unit once again, and then draw a mindmap of* Pride and Prejudice (*2005*).

☞ 2. Movie review

Direction: *Enjoy reading the movie review sample of* Gone with the Wind. *Scan the QR code for the movie review sample and addresses attached for your further study.*

References

☞ 1. Ways to practise retelling stories

Retelling is a skill that students have to practise over and over. But how do you keep it interesting if students must practise retelling repeatedly? There are engaging ways to practise retelling!

Ways to practise retelling stories

- **Give students a purpose for retelling**
  - Ask students questions to help they understand the importance of retelling.
    - Retelling is a great way to share information about a movie or text with other people.
    - Retelling is a good way to remember what you have read or watched, and check to make sure that you really understand a text.
  - Students need to understand why we ask them to do things.

- **Provide a predictable structure to set students up for success**
  - Asking students to "mentally organize" the parts of a story makes it easier for them to retell it.
  - Teach them to think about the beginning, the middle, and the end, and have them write or draw a picture or mindmap for each part.

- **Identify the theme**
  - A theme is the central idea in the story. It sums up what the story shows us about the human condition.
  - Be able to summarize it in a simple statement.

- **Respect students' individual preferences in ways of practising retelling**
  - Providing choice is a great motivator. Some students may want to draw, write, or talk it out with a friend. As long as they all learn to retell a story, let them choose how they get there.

☞ 2. How to improve your debate skills?

To meet the judge's criteria, you will have to develop certain debate skills. Consider the following.

Unit 18

Jane Eyre (2011)

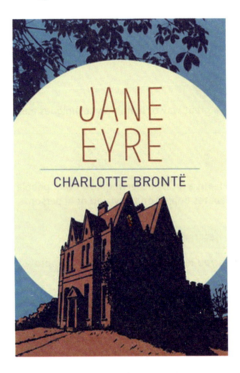

Unit Objectives:

1. Speaking skills:
   - Develop proficiency in public speaking through the use of effective retelling techniques, thereby improving communication and presentation skills.
   - Acquire the skills and techniques necessary to become a successful debater, allowing for the confident and effective expression of ideas and opinions.

2. Emotional objectives:
   - Cultivate an awareness of the importance of independence and self-reliance, encouraging students to take responsibility for their own actions and decisions.
   - Foster a healthy attitude towards beauty, emphasizing the need to appreciate inner qualities and values rather than external appearances alone.
   - Encourage self-discovery and personal growth, promoting a sense of exploration and curiosity in students with regards to their own talents, interests, and potential.

Section I Pre-class Tasks

The students are supposed to watch the movie of *Jane Eyre* (2011) for at least 2 or 3 times ahead of the class, the first time for general understanding of the movie, and the second and third times for more detailed understanding and learning of English language, and then complete the following tasks before the class time.

☞ 1. Classic movie lines

Direction: *Read and recite the following lines from the movie.*
(1) Intelligence and a proper education will give you ... independence of spirit. And that is the greatest blessing of all.
(2) Most true it is that "beauty is in the eye of the gazer".
(3) I care for myself. The more solitary, the more friendless, the more unsustained I am, the more I will respect myself.

☞ 2. Background knowledge

Direction: *Go through the passage and prepare to share the information in class.*

Jane, an orphan, lives with her uncle's family. Her parents died of typhus. She has been being maltreated and segregated by her aunt, Mr. Reed and her cousins for ten years. Finally she is sent to Lowood, a charity school, where she and the other girls are also mistreated. Although life is hard in Lowood, she grows to be confident and strong in will. She has been studying there since the age of ten, and becomes a teacher there when she grows up. Then she leaves Lowood to work as a governess at Thornfield Hall.

At Thornfield she meets Mrs. Alice Fairfax, the kindly housekeeper who comes to be Jane's friend. She tells Jane that her job is to teach and take care of Adele, the daughter of a French dancer who was one of the employer's mistresses. Jane's employer, Edward Rochester, is wealthy and impetuous. Jane falls in love with Mr. Rochester, but he is expected to marry Blanche Ingram, a snobbish woman. Mr. Rochester also falls in love with Jane and proposes to marry her. However, on their wedding day, Jane discovers a terrible and dark secret that Rochester cannot legally marry her, because he already has a wife, Bertha Mason, who has gone mad and is locked on the third floor. Jane leaves Thornfield.

After leaving Thornfiled, Jane is taken in by her cousin, St. John, a clergyman who later proposes to marry her. Jane refuses John's proposal and returns to Thornfield to see Rochester. Back at Thornfield, Jane finds the estate has been burned by Rochester's wife who has been killed herself after setting the fire; and that Rochester is blinded for trying to save her wife in the fire. At last Jane and Rochester get married.

3. Vocabulary

Direction: *Learn these new words and expression(s) from this movie and try to use them at EANLIC night.*

endure /ɪnˈdjʊə(r)/ *v.* to experience and deal with sth. that is painful or unpleasant, especially without complaining 忍耐,忍受

wretched /ˈretʃɪd/ *adj.* extremely bad or unpleasant 极坏的,恶劣的

willful /ˈwɪlfl/ *adj.* habitually disposed to disobedience and opposition 任性的

obstinate /ˈɒbstɪnət/ *adj.* refusing to change your opinions, way of behaving, etc. when other people try to persuade you to; showing this 执拗的;固执的;顽固的

wicked /ˈwɪkɪd/ *adj.* morally bad 邪恶的,缺德的

deceit /dɪˈsiːt/ *n.* dishonest behavior that is intended to make sb. believe that sth. is not true; an example of this behavior 欺骗,欺诈(行为);诡计

tolerate /ˈtɒləreɪt/ *v.* to allow sb. to do sth. that you do not agree with or like 容许,允许(不同意或不喜欢的事物)

befit /bɪˈfɪt/ *v.* to be suitable and good enough for sb./sth. 适合,对……相称

prospects /ˈprɒspekts/ *n.* the chances of being successful 成功的机会,前景,前途

humble /ˈhʌmbl/ *adj.* showing you do not think that you are as important as other people 谦逊的,虚心的

akin /əˈkɪn/ *adj.* similar to 相似的,类似的

tame /teɪm/ *v.* to make sth. tame or easy to control 驯化;驯服;使易于控制

chin /tʃɪn/ *n.* the part of the face below the mouth and above the neck 颏,下巴

poke /pəʊk/ *v.* to quickly push your fingers or another object into sb./sth. (用手指或其他东西)捅戳,杵

portrait /ˈpɔːtreɪt/ *n.* a painting, drawing or photograph of a person, especially of the head and shoulders 肖像;半身画像;半身照

defiance /dɪˈfaɪəns/ *n.* open refusal to obey sb./sth. 违抗,反抗,拒绝服从

decent /ˈdiːs(ə)nt/ *adj.* acceptable to people in a particular situation 得体的,合宜的,适当的

curl /kɜːl/ *v.* to form or make sth. form into a curl or curls 卷;(使)拳曲,鬈曲

offend /əˈfend/ *v.* to make sb. feel upset because of sth. you say or do that is rude or embarrassing 得罪,冒犯

vanity /ˈvænəti/ *n.* too much pride in your own appearance, abilities or achievements 自负;自大;虚荣;虚荣心

suppress /səˈpres/ *v.* to prevent yourself from having or expressing a feeling or an emotion 抑制,控制,忍住

matter /ˈmætə(r)/ *v.* to be important or have an important effect on sb./sth. 事关紧要,要紧,有重大影响

harmony /ˈhɑːməni/ *n.* a state of peaceful existence and agreement 融洽,和睦

bare /beə(r)/ *adj.* not covered by any clothes 裸体的,裸露的
grieve /griːv/ *v.* to feel very sad, especially because sb. has died (尤指因某人的去世而)悲伤,悲痛,伤心
stretch /stretʃ/ *v.* to put your arms or legs out straight and contract your muscles 伸展,舒展
tenacious /təˈneɪʃəs/ *adj.* that does not stop holding sth. or give up sth. easily/deter mined 紧握的,不松手的,坚持的

Expression(s)

keep an eye on   留意,密切注意
guard against   提防,防范

☞ 4. Character description

Direction: *Describe the main characters by using at least 5 adjectives in this movie with the reference of the words you have learned, and find examples in the movie to support your ideas (Table 18.1).*

Table 18.1   Main Characters in *Jane Eyre* (2011)

Main Characters	Adjectives	Examples
Jane Eyre		
St. John Rivers		
Rochester		
Mrs. Reed		
John Reed		
Helen Burns		
Mrs. Fairfax		
Adele		
Blanche Ingram		

Section II In-class Tasks

☞ 1. Workshop

Direction: *Discuss the questions with your classmates, and use the following sentence structures if it is possible.*

Sentence structures for higher level questions & changing the subject
- *Does this connect to ... that we have already learned?*

- What would happen if …?
- What effect would … have?
- How would … apply in this case?
- What information (idea) would support what … (name) is saying?
- Have we exhausted the topic of …? Is it okay if we move on to …?
- Does anyone have any final comments to add about … before we move on to …?

(1) Upon leaving Lowood, why does Jane feel she is abandoning Miss Temple?

(2) How does Helen die? What causes her death indeed?

(3) What can we infer about Lowood School when Rochester says "you must be tenacious of life to survive that place so long"?

(4) How does Jane react to Rochester's accusation that Jane's responsible for his sprain?

(5) How do you understand the sentence "that shadows are as important as the light"?

(6) What is Rochester's first impression of Jane?

2. Cloze

Direction: *Fill in the gaps in the following passages taken from the movie with the words or phrases given below.*

Passage 1

told	grave and quiet	wife	cleverly	the Rochester name	suitable match
law	violent lunacy	lunatic	better off	wished to have	kept away from
judge	torment	mad	prop up	what they wanted	

This is my ___1___ . Your sister, Mason. Look at her. She is ___2___ ! So was her mother. So was her grandmother. Three generations of ___3___ . I wasn't told about that, was I, Mason? All I was told about was that my father had made a ___4___ , one that would ___5___ his dwindling fortune and give your family ___6___ ! I did what I was ___7___ ! And Bertha was ___8___ me, until the wedding was ___9___ done. Everyone got ___10___ … except me. Even she is ___11___ here than she would be in a ___12___ asylum, but I have spent the last fifteen years in ___13___ ! And this what I, what I ___14___ . This young girl who stands so ___15___ at the mouth of hell. Look at the difference. Then ___16___ me, priest on the gospel and man of the ___17___ , and remember with what judgment ye judge, ye … Off with you now.

Passage 2

a proper education	grow	intelligence	independence of spirit
matters	blessed	in harmony with	very sorry for yourselves
cut off	greatest	more beautiful	envy	hair

Your ___1___ will grow again soon. And if it's ___2___ again, it will ___3___ again. And it will be even ___4___ than it was before. Come, into bed.

I'm sure you feel ___5___. I'm sure you all ___6___ other girls who seem to have been ___7___ with happier lives. But you have all been blessed with ___8___. Intelligence and ___9___ will give you ___10___. And that is the ___11___ blessing of all. The only thing that ___12___ in your life, is to be ___13___ God.

☞ 3. Story retelling

Direction: *Study the information on five storytelling techniques in Reference 1, and then retell the story of* Jane Eyre *(2011) by using specific details to support your ideas (Table 18.2).*

Table 18.2 Five Storytelling Techniques to Become a Better Speaker

Five Storytelling Techniques	Your Notes
Tell a personal story	
Make the characters relatable	
Use emotions	
Use dialogues	
Cut unnecessary details	

☞ 4. Sentence rearrangement

Direction: *Put the following sentences into the chronological order based on the story of* Jane Eyre *(2011) (Table 18.3).*

Table 18.3 Sentences from *Jane Eyre* (2011)

Orders	Sentences
	You must be tenacious of life to survive that place so long. No wonder you have the look of another world about you.
	We are truly devoted, my Edward and I; our hearts beat as one; our happiness is complete.
	How can you be so stupid? How can you be so cruel? Just because I'm poor and plain, I'm not without feelings.
	Well, you know what they say, "lucky at cards; unlucky in love".
	How can you be so stupid? How can you be so cruel? Just because I'm poor and plain, I'm not without feelings.

continued

Orders	Sentences
	Jane, you're a strange and almost unearthly thing.
	I once had a heart full of tender feelings. But fortune has knocked me about. Now I'm hard and tough as an India rubber ball.
	My parents died when I was very young. I went to stay with my Aunt who didn't love me.
	There are painful memories which are perhaps best forgotten.
	You can always tell a governess at first glance. They're plain in a very special way.

Section III English Chat Task

Direction: *Discuss the themes of this movie and organize your words on the specific themes (Table 18.4).*

Table 18.4 Themes of *Jane Eyre* (2011)

Themes	Questions about Themes	Answers (Key Words for Each Question)
Love and marriage	• Why does Rochester marry Bertha? • For what does Rochester love Jane?	
Independence of women	• What's the difference between Helen and Jane? • Why does Jane leave Rochester when she knows that he is married?	
Wealth and marriage	• Who is Blanche Ingram? • Why does she want to marry Rochester?	

Section IV EANLIC Party Tasks

☞ **1. Give a presentation on the theme of *Jane Eyre* (2011)**

☞ **2. Role-play**

Direction: *Prepare this part in groups before class, and then do the role-play in class. Scan the QR code for role-play scripts.*

(1) The night Helen is dying.
(2) Rochester talks on Jane's sketches.

☞ 3. Debate

Direction: *Study the debate information in Reference 2 of this unit, and deliver a debate confidently and effectively.*

(1) Does Jane's return to Rochester after she inherits a fortune demonstrate that Jane loves herself more than Rochester?

For: Jane's return to Rochester after she inherits a fortune demonstrates that Jane loves herself more than Rochester.

Against: Jane's return to Rochester after she inherits a fortune can't lead to the conclusion that Jane loves herself more than Rochester.

(2) Should college students prioritize romantic relationships over academic pursuits?

For: College students should seek for romantic relationships first.

Against: College students should prioritize academic pursuits.

Section V After-class Tasks

☞ 1. Mindmap drawing

Direction: *Read Reference 1 of this unit once again, and then draw a mindmap of* Jane Eyre.

☞ 2. Movie review

Direction: *Enjoy reading the movie review sample of* Gone with the Wind. *Scan the QR code for the movie review sample and addresses attached for your further study.*

References

☞ 1. Five storytelling techniques to become a better speaker

When was the last time that you experienced a very compelling speaker? Do you remember what you liked about the story? Were there any elements that you found particularly interesting?

All the storytellers were having been put in rigorous practice to get to where they are. They use specific techniques to become more engaging, more inspirational and more memorable. Everyone can learn the techniques to become a better storyteller. Good storytelling offers a route to the heart, sticks longer in the mind, and will leave a call to action that delivers results. Here are 5 storytelling techniques that will transform your stories.

Five storytelling techniques to become a better speaker

Tell a personal story

Why it matters

Create the same level of connection on people for a personal story is inspiring, motivative, and influencial.

How you do it

Tell a personal story about a challenge that you faced in your life and how you overcame it.

Make sure that the lesson learned is relevant to your audience.

Make the characters relatable

Why it matters

Tell a story about an extreme event (like a near-death experience) would be interesting.

How you do it

Make it relatable if you want your audience to remember your story and act upon it. Pick a character that the audience can identify or familiarize.

Communicate a challenge or struggle that the audience can relate to.

Use emotions

Why it matters

Emotions are the main reasons why we remember things.

Bring emotions into your story, if you want to affect behavior and change mindsets.

How you do it

Reactions: Show how the character reacts physically and emotionally to the obstacle.

Inner monologue: Show the character's inner monologue that the character has with himself/ herself in silence. Recreating your inner monologue draws the audience in and makes them feel like they were listening in during your thought processes.

Pause: Pause and feel the moment for a few seconds, when something surprising happens in your story.

Use dialogues

Why it matters

Turn a dry story into a more relatable story with real people by adding dialogue between two characters to your story. Make you sound more conversational.

How you do it

Make sure to include a dialogue in your story when the character encounters the challenge.

Try to speak as if you were the other character to make it even more interesting for your audience.

Cut unnecessary details

Why it matters

Most leadership stories fall into the range of 3-5mins; therefore, every word that you use should serve a very specific purpose.

How you do it

Don't hesitate to take a sentence or phrase that doesn't add value to you story.

Review every single sentence in your story and ask yourself : "Does it help in any way to deliver my message?" or "Does it help to make my story more engaging ?"

☞ 2. How to be a better debater?

Learning how to debate helps students develop critical thinking, language, and teamwork skills. A few simple rules apply to be a better debater. When you use effective communication, a well-placed argument, and really pay attention to what your opponent is saying, you can make just about any opinion sound like the right one.

How to be a better debater?

Communicate effectively

- **Follow the form**
  - Follow a format in formal debates, and you'll want to know that formula like the back of your hand so that you're prepared. It's also important because breaking from the formula can lose you points.

- **Keep calm**
  - Stay calm when you debate. Keep your voice even and keep your facial expression neutral. This makes it much harder for your opponent to find what buttons they can press to make you trip up.

- **Speak clearly**
  - Speak clearly when you talk so that people can understand you. It also makes you sound smarter and more confident. Speak clearly by using a loud enough volume that people can hear you and then enunciate your words.

- **Explain your logic**
  - Explain your logic to someone how you arrived at the conclusion, and you guide them to think in the same way that yours does. As long as your reasoning is at least good on the surface, this can be one of the most effective ways to bring someone over to your side of the argument.

- **Be respectful and fair**
  - Be respectful when you argue with someone. Don't insult them, talk over them, or judge them. You should also be fair in an argument. Don't distort the facts. Use evidence against them that is recent and directly related.

- **Act confidently**
  - Acting confidently can make you and your argument much more appealing and believable. Make eye contact with your opponent, as well as people in your audience also can make youself more confident.

Choose your arguments

- **Use arguments based on logic**
  - Use examples and ideas which are rooted in simple, direct reasoning. This is helpful when debating with someone who considers themselves smart and logical.

- **Use arguments based on emotions**
  - Use appeals to people's heart and emotions. This is helpful when debating with someone who is prone to strong emotions (showing heightened joy and easily visible sadness).

- **Use arguments based on authority**
  - Use appeals to your authority and credibility or that of another who supports your ideas. This is helpful when debating with someone who is not as experienced in the field or who has a particularly weak argument.

Win a debate

- **Do your research**
  - Do your research if you want to guarantee a win as much as possible. The more prepared you are for a debate, the better you'll do. When you know a topic backwards and forwards and from all angles, you'll be much better prepared to counter any argument your opponent might dream up.

- **Look for logical fallacies**
  - Pointing out logical fallacies in your opponent's argument makes you look better. You force them to either accept them and reduce the credibility of their argument. It also requires them to use their precious time to try and argue that their argument isn't illogical.

- **Look for weaknesses in their argument**
  - Find and point out the weaknesses in your opponent's argument make yours look stronger by comparison.

- **Keep the topic on track**
  - Keep an argument on track and you'll be more likely to win. Ask yourself if the current argument ties directly back to the topic you're supposed to be dealing with. If it doesn't support one side or the other, the argument is off track.

参考文献

1. Bailey, K.M. *Practical English Language Teaching：Speaking* [M]. Nunan, D (Ed.). Beijing：Tsinghua University Press, 2013.
2. Ellis, R. *The Study of Second Language Acquisition* [M]. 2nd. Oxford：Oxford University Press, 2008.
3. Harmer, J. *How to Teach English* [M]. Beijing：Foreign Language Teaching and Research Press, 2000.
4. Lynn, Andrew. 英语电影赏析[M]. 北京：外语教学与研究出版社, 2005.
5. Nunan, D. *Task-based Language Teaching* [M]. Cambridge：Cambridge University Press, 2004.
6. Nunan, D. *Teaching English to Speakers of Other Languages：An Introduction* [M]. London, New York：Routledge, 2015.
7. Woodward, T. *Planning Lessons and Courses* [M]. Cambridge：Cambridge University Press, 2001.
8. 方映, 刘蕾. 英语影视赏析[M]. 天津：天津大学出版社, 2011.
9. 李超, 蒋晖. 英语影视视听说教程(1)学生用书[M]. 上海：上海外语教育出版社, 2015.
10. 吉乐, 李雪梅. 经典影视赏析[M]. 西安：西安交通大学出版社, 2012.
11. 庞维国. 自主学习：学与教的原理和策略[M]. 上海：华东师范大学出版社, 2003.
12. 王蔷. 英语教学法教程[M]. 2版. 北京：高等教育出版社, 2006.
13. 徐锦芬. 现代外语教学的理论与实践[M]. 武汉：华中科技大学出版社, 2006.
14. 徐锦芬, 刘文波. 实用英语教学法教程[M]. 北京：中国人民大学出版社, 2019.
15. 徐泉, 王婷. 英语教学技能训练教程[M]. 上海：上海外语教育出版社, 2018.

参考答案　　资料出处